REFLECTIONS on *Life*

AF657899

LUBHITA SHEKHAWAT

BlueRoseONE.com
Stories Matter
NewDelhi • London

BLUEROSE PUBLISHERS
India | U.K.

BlueRose ONE
Stories Matter
NewDelhi • London

For permissions requests or inquiries regarding this publication, please contact:

BLUEROSE PUBLISHERS
www.BlueRoseONE.com
info@bluerosepublishers.com
+91 8882 898 898
+4407342408967

ISBN: 978-93-6452-169-7

Cover design: Yash Singhal
Typesetting: Namrata Saini

First Edition: February 2025

Disclaimer

All images featured in this book, with the exception of the family photographs, have been sourced from Google and other publicly accessible online platforms to align with the content and thematic requirements of the book. These images are used solely for illustrative purposes and are not owned by the author. The author does not hold any copyright or proprietary rights to these images, and they are included without the intent to infringe upon any intellectual property rights. Should any image require attribution or removal, please contact us for appropriate action.

Dedicated to the living memory of

My Parents...

Karanpal Singh & Lalima Singh

Thank you for teaching me everything

Thank you for the Love you gave me

I know you two are together now,looking over us.

Acknowledgement

Quite a lot goes into creating something of value. Memories, love, guidance, advice, upbringing, education, family, friends and experiences have made it possible for me to put forward this collection of my blogs written over a period of twelve-thirteen years.

Those who have contributed need to be acknowledged & cherished.

My parents for teaching me everything good I know.

My sisters, Vatsala & Takshna, for being examples of stoic courage and always being present for me.

My adorable niece Mishti and two great nephews, Raghu & Shubhu, for being the reasons I live for.

My friends for always having my back.

Sujata di for being my friend, mentor & guide and for letting me use her tribute to her mother in this book.

Rahul, Neha, Jitesh & Ajay for being my subject matters more than once & for the Love that I have unabashedly received from them over the years.

Vishal ji for letting me know what not to and how not to write. (You do get the pun)

The written word.. books.. which I believe are magic, for getting me enchanted early in my life.

GRATEFUL..

Foreword

My association with Lubhita is almost a decade and a half long and in the interim we have forged a bond that has only grown stronger with time.

I have seen Lubhita evolve splendidly over the years from a reticent, slightly shy young person to the poised, supremely confident woman that she is today. Her prose reflects this amazing trajectory which comes as no surprise to those who know her. She has experienced the vicissitudes of life at an age which most people go without their entire lives. The pain and trauma, the irreparable loss of those who were her raison d' etre have all gone into her writing in a way that it impacts the readers at a very personal level.

The colours of life are sometimes dim, at others, vibrant but Lubhita chooses to create her own palette in a manner that can only be called inimitable. Her blogs have a clarity of expression; there is a fluidity to the words that seems unforced and totally uncontrived. Above all, there is an honesty in her commentaries and POVs on issues, on relationships and on the myriad shades that make up our lives.

I will be one, among her many happy readers, when she begins to wield her pen once again.

Sujata Bhatt

Friend, mentor and guide

Contents

The Uncertainty of Life

September 20, 2010

It is indeed a difficult subject to take up right at the beginning of my blogging life but my day today led me to open my eyes to the uncertainty of human life.

This morning when I reached my school, it is where I teach, I found my colleagues discussing the accidental death of a family. What made it all the more heartbreaking was the fact that one of our students (ours is a residential school) had visitors this Sunday. Her parents and brother had come to visit her. 15 mins after they left her in the campus they met with a fatal accident. All of them died a sudden and terrible death. Little did the child realise that her parents would never laugh with her again, that her brother would never tease her and never would she experience that unbinding love ever again.

And to think that last night I was worried about something as irrelevant to living as a lost boyfriend.

Wish I could do something to relieve her of her pain.

New Day

September 21, 2010

It is yet another day. Optimists would insist on it being a new day.

I, on my part, am glad to have lived to see one more.

It is difficult to sort out the numerous thoughts going around in my head right now. It's such a jumble. I would need a lot of practice to be able to sound coherent in my blogs especially when I intend writing to be my catharsis.

Yesterday's incident had me thinking..

mine is not the biggest problem in the world

People do survive worse hits too.

Mom always says, you can't die of disappointments and while you are breathing it's always good to live it up rather than drag it down.

Advice taken at least for today

No more long faces.

I have work to do…

I think this would work for me.

Charactersssssss

September 21, 2010

I have not gone and thrown my sense of English to trash with the kind of title you read. My piece today deals with the various characters one comes across through the day.This is especially true for people who have the chance to interact with loads of people in their worksphere.

Interesting to note, if we pay attention nearly all human beings are full of contradictions. I have never ever come across a person who would say , ‘ fine this is my mistake.’ without providing explanations as to why they were forced to act in a certain way. We are never ever wrong. What is wrong is others’ perception of us. We all have separate sets of rules for anyone other than our good selves. It's amazing how and why people quarrel and confront each other when the basic style of thinking and reacting is the same. We often see that a criminal understands and vouches for others involved in crime, a student understands the pressures of other students no matter where they study, an employee sympathises with the grievance of workers everywhere yet we fail to unite under our common identity – HUMANITY..

Choices...

September 23, 2010

If we are born as humans we are sure to have some qualities and some weak points. Every human has been accorded a chance to build upon whichever side they feel comfortable with. We very often fall into the trap of pumping the wrong side of our personality. It is a human failing which is quite common but then again you don't need to be a super human to see the brighter side of your character and flaunt that to the world. I have seen people around me who are not extraordinary by birth but their clear vision, set principles, flexible beliefs, sweet nature and most importantly the power to read and understand themselves make them successful in whatever they do. They are liked by others, seen as a source of inspiration by many and, what is more important is that, they don't have to strive to be happy or look for reasons to smile. Living is their reason for pleasure. It's not that turmoils don't hit them but they take them in their stride. For them it is true 'can victory be as sweet when we have had no failures'. Positive thinking comes easily to them. They don't have to train their minds around the various phases of life. Life grows and they flow along with it. In the end it all comes down to the choices we make in life. Let us choose to be happy and develop a caring attitude for people who have always been there in our lives, loving us despite all our shortcomings. Let me value those who value and love me beyond any reason. Today and forever..

Whose fault is it anywaz.........

September 23, 2010

Nothing is sadder than witnessing the fall of a titan.

Painstakingly built, it is unnerving to see an establishment crumbling down to dust. In the figurative sense of course.

I sat pondering over its sad demise today and unsurprisingly I realised that the answer was right in front of us all the time but we failed to see. As we failed to realise our own contribution in its disintegration.

Feudal ideology was not without essence, you see. When monarchs ruled they took advice from their ministers. A king who failed to win the loyalty of his subordinates and subjects, couldn't make an impression on history. The same stands true for today's time too. A leader should be able to judge who his/her assets are. People who would gladly give up anything to fulfill your wishes and commands, need to be appreciated and recognised. They need to be told how important they are. A leader has to open his eyes and judge for himself.

The fate of an institution depends on sound leadership. Just being a wonderful human being won't suffice. I am not a management guru but this little mantra of survival might save my empire (I am merely a subject of the empire) from the doom it is headed for.. Amen

Solitude

September 29, 2010

It is said that life teaches you at every stage. We are learners all our lives. One learns to live with the trials and turbulences of our being but what is difficult to overcome is the SOLITUDE. It is difficult to find someone who can be considered your soulmate, yet again, not all soulmates turn out to be together for life. What happens once such a soulmate leaves your life??????

It is difficult to think and more so to cope up with. You may be distracted with time but does that pain ever wither down? Somebody sent me an interesting message which goes like this—-

I have seen castles made out of sand, met people who believe
That destiny is engraved on the palm of their hands…
I have seen people change their faith,

Experienced love which turns into hate…
I have seen some grow younger with age,

and a bird who won't fly out of an open cage….
I have seen love sold for money,
people who are devastated inside but outside they are funny…..

I have seen a unicorn fall in love with a toad,
people who owned half the city have now hit the road…
I have learnt to expect the unexpected,
perfection doesn't exist, we all are born defected…
everyone cries, some just hide their tears,
they say coal turns into diamond over a thousand years…
for some you are just another nobody in a million,
but for someone you are one in a million…
What if that one in a million goes away?

Speaking from experience, life never comes to a stand still. It goes on.. and we learn to love it once again. Solitude is not natural. It may be there for a stretched period of time but doesn't last forever. Nothing lasts forever. Change is the rule of life. And life is for the living. I know it's a disoriented piece of writing. I just don't want to miss out on any of my emotions

Loss….

November 26, 2010

It kills to realise that something one has put a lot of effort in, is lost. Today I was fortunate enough to judge a declamation contest in which, though, the speakers were not very inspiring, one topic caught my attention. Take care of the small things in life and the big things will all fall into place on their own. The speaker went about citing examples from everyday life. Say an obese person trying to get into shape has to make small efforts to achieve what at the onset might look a mammoth task. I know and realise that all this is right and has to be done to maintain a semblance of normalcy but how would you explain it to someone who has invested, say, all her life in building up a dream and then watched it shatter in front of her eyes? There are people who live through worse circumstances in life and survive beautifully. Such people are exemplary. But does the pain of loss ever die? You may move ahead but it remains with you wherever you go, whatever you do. I don't understand how the philosophy of taking care of small things apply in this case. I am clueless how to deal with a loss. For some it may be a natural trick of survival, I guess I am slow there…

Motherhood.....

December 9, 2010

People say that MOTHERHOOD completes a woman. I had never thought I would come to believe something as basic as that. I have seen so many births in the family that they have stopped affecting me. Infact I don't remember ever being moved by the feeling of bringing a new life into this world.

For me, it has always been routine. One of those things that exists and has minimum impact on me or how I live. It was so, till this morning. Then, my sister gave birth to a baby boy.

I won't go as far as saying that it changed my perspective or vision but indeed it gave me an insight on selfless love. For ages now, I have been using the word EXHILARATED....without actually knowing how it feels to be so. Today I got lucky to sense this emotion too. Of Course I couldn't understand why my heart was palpitating so much or why my breath couldn't settle for a long time after I heard the nurse break the news to the family but now nearly 12 hours after it all happened, I am grateful that I have lived to experience something as pure and moving as this.

I couldn't help but notice that sharing the good news with someone who is completely there with you makes it all the more special and easier to digest. I, unfortunately, did not have anyone to share what I felt. So I am pouring my heart out here for all to read.

May God be kind enough to provide all around me with such special pleasures and most importantly PEOPLE to share them with..... AMEN

Frailty thy Name is....MAN

January 10, 2011

It's surprising to see how fast a person retreats into one's inner cocoon when faced with the harsh realities of life. Nothing breaks a spirit like LONELINESS. This is true for all humans. We are weak by nature. Only our inner self has that store house of courage which shows us the way even in the darkest hours of our lives. Not everyone is strong or patient enough to extract that which is latent in us. It is amusing to note that we need the support of our fellow humans, be it in the capacity of friends, family or spouse, to play this game called life, at every step, on all occasions, every moment. We can't be alone. Even those who are seemingly strong are so due to the support of their loved ones. All said and done, the basic attribute of MAN is frailty..

Man- An island..

May 14, 2011

I vividly remember a phrase I had read way back in my childhood in a book or a journal, I don't remember which, but one which has stayed with me ever since.. "He had become an ISLAND". The metaphorical import of these words was lost on me. Now at this stage in my life I understand every syllable of it. There comes a time in our lives when we become islands, all of us. It is when either age stands in our way of understanding the new trends of the world or when we confine ourselves to what we once were, unable or unwilling to accept what we have become now. This is the same as ignorance is bliss like what people think of me and my attitude is their problem not mine kind of philosophy. As islands can't survive all alone, men can't too. We need human company to survive and for that we have to accept the realities of our world. Live and let others live.

This feeling of seclusion is worst when it creeps into our lives in the most intimate fashion. Distances between husband-wives, parents-children, siblings, friends. The silence hurts and damages beautiful relationships irreparably.

Don"t be the harbinger of this kind of living hell. Learn to love and share. If you have to be something, be a river which moves tirelessly and joins the all consuming sea losing its identity for love.... CEASE BEING AN ISLAND...

A man is what time makes him.....

August 2, 2011

A tight corner in life or any hardship which doesn't kill us makes us stronger. A man after all, is the outcome of his circumstances.Today, dad got talking about his childhood and his beginnings. There is so much to be learnt from the lives of our elders. I feel the thing that is missing in us, the younger generation, is a sense of belonging. We hardly realise where we come from, our ROOTS so to say. Successful, popular and well known that he is, my dad still remembers the suffering, struggle and sacrifice of his elder siblings and love & care of relatives and other people in his village, though he was still a kid when all that happened. It's heartwarming and inspiring to know that he remembers, cares and is deeply concerned for the kith and kin of all those who were there for him when he, a sick motherless toddler, wanted care. Times have changed bringing with them prosperity and every luxury that money can afford but dad, simpleton that he is, still values people more than the conveniences of life. Nearly half a century after he saw his elder sister, a motherless teen herself, looking after him and his two younger siblings, he is still moved to tears recalling her unspoken anguish at being served a raw deal by fate, her own childhood burnt to cinders in the fire of the hearth. He recalls the silent yet determined presence of his young uncle at his bedside when he was suffering from an acute bout of smallpox and how his resilience and belief nursed my dad back to health. He remembers how his maternal grandpa took them all under his wing once his mother passed away. The dismal picture of poverty and want that dad paints, is beyond imagination. Today he is what he is, as a result of the hardships that he has experienced. The strength of his character shines as he has waded the troubled waters of life and come up on merit, still never forgetting the past. The indelible imprint of time makes him my ideal.

Are we ANNA?

August 18, 2011

The entire nation is engulfed today in an anti- corruption mood, a mass movement of this proportion had never been thought of in independent India..one man ANNA HAZARE has managed to accomplish something that the collective might of political parties and our elected representatives had failed so far to do - to bring India together like this on one issue is indeed a commendable feat. His lack of political ambition and selfless devotion to a larger good has led us to compare Anna with Bapu. We, in India, had come to believe that mass movements like this are just subject matters of textbooks. Not any more. Nevertheless, riding high on wave ANNA and in their eagerness to play a part in the first ever mass movement post independence, Indians have, however, overlooked one tiny problem- the issue, which is still CORRUPTION. With a war cry of "I AM ANNA" or "main ANNA hoon", are we to believe that the entire nation is a group of innocent, system tired individuals who have never indulged in corruption at any point of time. Even if we exclude people who have bribed more than once, unwillingly, due to the system, we will still find that most people standing in ANNA's favour today are the very same who have shamelessly accepted bribes or favors or misused their positions in one way or the other. Can we, then, put all the blame on the elected few and consider our duty done? Can we ever refrain from government bashing? It isn't the government's pleasure to deny the demands of an indefinite fast and public meeting to ANNA and his followers, it is their duty, entrusted to them by us, to maintain law & order in the nation. Can anyone guarantee that in a country so full of contradictions and volatile temperaments, a public meeting will not turn violent? Is the government then wrong in putting the restrictions that we are so vehemently opposing today? What we are witnessing today is ANNARCHY… people who don't even realise the true import of ANNA's demands are behind him today, displaying once again our allegiance to MOBOCRACY, a tendency that our democracy has taken to, over the years. Should ANNA not, in the true spirit of Gandhigiri, implore his followers today to analyse & examine their actions too before they can usurp the right to criticise the system & the government? Can a system be corrupt without its individual units being so? And who makes the system if not the people? By all means SUPPORT ANNA but question the system only if you have never faulted on corruption in the past or have vowed never to indulge in it in future. All said and done, we are in a dire need of bills such as Lokpal to make our democracy function as it was meant to but what we REALLY need today are good, sincere and honest citizens who can peep into their conscience and not feel guilty or shame faced about anything that has transpired through them for the Nation. We might not be ANNA today but we certainly hope to become HIM someday…

"The Man" stands tall....

July 25, 2012

Every once in a while we come across a book which inspires us to be what we ought to be and not just what we are expected to be. Irving Wallace's 'The Man' gives us more. No book lover can remain unmoved by the sheer brilliance of characterization and plot. The fluidity of events which take place in the life of His Accidency (pun intended) The President of the United States Douglass Dilman, the first amongst his race to reach this high office by an accident of fate, is unnerving.

Written in the 1960s, 'The Man' is the story of a black man who succeeds to the White House as a result of the untimely and unfortunate death of the elected President. Resented by nearly all his cabinet members, the white house staff and the skeptical and aggrieved people of the country, Douglass Dilman emerges a victor and true leader of his people who are not just blacks.

The inner dilemmas and demons of a Negro in post civil war America have been laid out in simple yet vivid and compelling language. The Man portrays the daily battle for existence and equality which an Afro-American had to contend with in those spiteful days. When faced with his impeachment the true grit and mettle of The Man comes forth.

The novel underlines the fact that –

Right is Right, it is not black, white, yellow or blue…

Beginning with a note of uncertainty about the impact his color and race would bear on the Presidency, Douglass Dilman reaches out and touches the hearts and lives of all those who know him and even those who don't.

Compulsive reading…

"Fight your demons..never bow down…stand tall", says The Man..

Fine balance, indeed...

August 25, 2012

Turning the last pages of 'Fine Balance' by Rohinton Mistry, I realized once again what a moving story and brilliant characterization can achieve. The story revolves around a gamut of characters set in 'Emergency India'. Not only does it shatter various myths regarding the most important post Independence event but also brings the reader face to face with the stark reality of the nation that is India.

The author has been successful in converting the banalities of life into something worth considering. 21st century readers would be jolted out of their reveries when they are made to confront the naked reality of caste excesses in rural India, the police and government tamasha in the country, the Goondaraaj, the misuse of law & power, the corruption which is rampant at every level. One might feel "what is new here? we have seen and experienced all that.."

Enters the magic of the author.. The simplicity, with which he has spun the characters around all these threads to weave out a heady yarn, is breathtaking. One keeps waiting for pleasant tidings but the author's warning of a tragic ending at the beginning of the novel is to be taken seriously.

We are used to our stories being the tales of strong men who face all adversities and come out victorious at the end. Everyone lived happily ever after is supposed to be our favorite punchline. The author means to differ. His characters are strong men and women who are tossed, turned, tried, tested and finally broken by life. Happiness, if any, is short lived but enough for the readers and the characters to hang on to and crave for more.

The contrast of the life and death of a college student with the two low caste chamars turned tailors hits you between the eyes. The former leads a comparatively cocooned life. His troubles are more a misunderstanding of the younger generation with their parents. The unfortunate tailors, on the other hand, have been dealt a raw deal by fate. Loss is their middle name. Yet the strength of their characters makes one believe in life and its struggles. The only disappointing turn in the story is when the college student, in a daze of helplessness and loss, commits suicide. Some would support his decision..but that's just putting an end to his own misery without a thought for others who loved him. My heart went out to the tailors who had preferred to live rather than give in..

To be truthful, the novel made me thank God for the easy and comfortable life that He has bestowed on me. It made me realize the importance of inner strength and balance of mind and soul.

The characters in the novel keep repeating that 'everything ends badly' but it doesn't have to.. not always..

The book struck a chord deep inside.. a melancholy tune reverberated the innards of my heavy heart.

The Present...

September 24, 2012

This isn't a movie review. Just a little something I liked in the film 'Midnight in Paris'. It could have been set anywhere on the globe but it had to be in the most alluring and vivid example of human will and endeavor- Paris. The film captures the ethereal beauty of the captivating city of lights in a truly heartwarming and sepia tinted frame.

Dealing with the protagonist's profound love and passion for this enchanting city, the movie, however, addresses a deeper issue too- what many would term as Escapism, a concept not entirely alien to all of us belonging to the human race.

At some point or other in our lives, we all feel the urge to escape the present and head for a time which, according to our beliefs, is the Golden Era of human civilization. Sometimes this quest is not as lofty as it sounds and deals with just the mundane.

In a hilarious turn of events, the lead character of the story- a Hollywood scriptwriter turned struggling novelist, having escaped the truth of his engagement to someone who doesn't share his passions for the city of his dreams, finds himself in Paris of the 20's.

To his initial bewilderment and later pleasure, his midnight strolls through the city turn into an adventurous setting for rendezvous with all his artistic heroes beginning from Cole Porter, Scott Fitzgerald, Ernest Hemmingway, Pablo Picasso to Gertrude Stein. He even manages to get his manuscript critiqued by Stein.

Along the way he realizes the importance of his present and the hazards of delving into nostalgic fantasy.

He finally sets his life to order and begins to find happiness in the present.

The film gives a strong yet subtle message that life cannot be led in fantasies. We cannot always turn to a rosy past in order to escape today's reality. Present is what we have. Past is gone, done for, something to learn from not something to dwell on. We don't live there anymore. We have all been blessed with the gift of today, that's why it is the Present.

Nostalgia..

April 14, 2013

This morning I was looking for something. Not finding it, I decided to open my childhood cupboard, the one whose use I had given up years back. I just remembered that it was full of childhood junk of all kinds and loads of audio cassettes, which of course are now obsolete with song downloading & online music the latest trend. For years now I hadn't thought of its content, hadn't realized what a treasure trove of lost time, innocence & pleasure it would be.

I, naturally, forgot what I was initially looking for when I came across numerous small bits of paper with my scrawny illegible hand on them, bits of discarded and broken toys, pebbles yes!!!! Pebbles (I fail to comprehend the lure and love for these small stones for a person any age and yet I couldn't throw them out even today).

Finally I came across a bag full of old letters. Letters from friends and a very special teacher I once had. I couldn't help reading them all. Laughed at some, tried to remember the events so vividly explained in some, guffawed aloud at the things which seemed so important to a teenage girl and yet to me were beyond funny today. All the while I had this peculiar and very satisfying feeling of watching my life unfold before me through those letters. A kind of calm descended on me. I was transported to a time which though is just 15 years old, but seems like a lifetime.

In one of the letters, my friend was trying to tear out of the fold to scold me for not picking up the landline because she herself had taken the trouble to go to an S.T.D booth just to be able to say a simple hello. Some friends took out time to write weekly and reading their letters made me realize that even I had written to them frequently.

The simplicity of times gone by stared me in the eye. None of us had imagined that life could change so drastically within a decade. Who could have imagined the cell phones, the emails, messages on the go, skype(for god's sake)!!!!

My heart yearns for that simple, honest life. We have come a long way since then, not all bad I would say, but the personal touch is somewhat lost.

Such is the power of a letter. Even if we happen to read it decades after it was written, it still brings an honest, guileless smile to us.

India's tryst with destiny

August 15, 2013

Help the Refugees

The Hindustan Times

INDIA INDEPENDENT : BRITISH RULE ENDS

CONSTITUENT ASSEMBLY TAKES OVER

MOUNTBATTEN'S APPOINTMENT AS GOVERNOR-GENERAL ENDORSED

COLOURFUL CEREMONY MARKS BIRTH OF NATION

NEW STAR RISES IN THE EAST

LEADERS TELL NATION OF TASKS AHEAD

Governors Sworn In As Free India Is Born

HOMAGE TO THE FATHER OF THE NATION

THE NEW CABINET

Blessed Dawn of Independence!

Long Live Free India!

In Bereavement...

December 18, 2014

The Smallest Coffins are the Heaviest...

No child deserves to have his life cut short in such an inhuman gruesome manner. It is not fate or an act of God that snatched away the innocent children from their parents. It is a barbaric act perpetrated by human beings against their own kind.

The violence, that tore through Peshawar's Army Public School and bereaved not only the 130+ families but an entire nation, shocked and stunned every sane person on this planet, has got to be an eye- opener for all those who support, finance and preach this lunacy termed Jihad- the religious war.

Whose religion is this anyway? Which religion propagates this kind of hatred and cowardice? Is this an act of courage?

No, it is an act of mayhem carried out to create an atmosphere of fear, insecurity and terror in order to serve the narrow purposes of a select few. The perpetrators are not men of principle or religion because no religion sanctions such diabolical and demonic activities.

The newspapers and news channels are plastered with heart-rending images of the school in shambles, the walls scraped raw by bullet marks, the innocent blood spilt so recklessly, the memories of unfinished childhood nipped in the bud and a nation in mourning.

My heart goes out to the many mothers who have lost their children in the dastardly attack of December 16th, 2014. The irreparable loss of life and its inherent dreams that they would have to carry all their lives might turn out to be a burden too heavy for most of them.

No words will ever be able to fill the void left by this highly condemnable undertaking against guileless children.

Nida Fazli, a renowned poet and believer writes-

हर बार ये इल्ज़ाम रह गया..!

हर काम में कोई काम रह गया..!!

नमाज़ी उठ उठ कर चले गये मस्ज़िदों से..!

दहशतगरों के हाथ में इस्लाम रह गया..!!

खून किसी का भी गिरे यहां

नस्ल-ए-आदम का खून है आखिर

बच्चे सरहद पार के ही सही

किसी की छाती का सुकून है आखिर

ख़ून के नापाक ये धब्बे, ख़ुदा से कैसे छिपाओगे?

मासूमों के क़ब्र पर चढ़कर, कौन से जन्नत जाओगे?

कागज़ पर रख कर रोटियाँ, खाऊँ भी तो कैसे . . . . खून से लथपथ आता है, अखबार भी आजकल .

दिलेरी का हरगिज़ हरगिज़ ये काम नहीं है

दहशत किसी मज़हब का पैगाम नहीं है ....!

तुम्हारी इबादत, तुम्हारा खुदा, तुम जानो..

हमें पक्का यकीन है ये कतई इस्लाम नहीं है....!!

Isn't it time, for the human race, to forgive and forget past excesses and move forward? Let not misguided religious bigotry rob us of a chance for a peaceful and safer tomorrow.

Let HOPE not die an untimely death like the victims of this ghastly massacre.

Long Road Home...

May 21, 2015

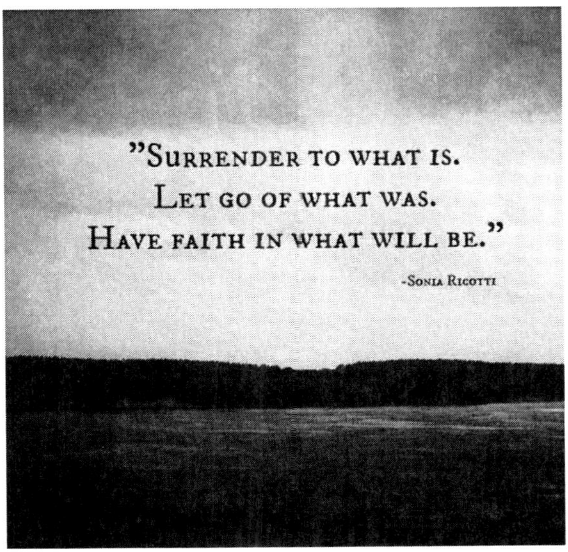

I entered my Bank this morning to an unfamiliar face in the manager's cabin. Engrossed deeply in his papers, he lacked familiarity & warmth. My eyes began looking for our regular 'Manager Sahab', found him sitting on a desk in the dark recesses of the Bank. I made a beeline for him. He looked up from his computer screen, saw me. A wise sad smile creased his weather-beaten face. To my silent question he glanced at his old cabin and said, " I am here for just another week, my replacement is already here. You won't find me here on your next visit." I, not deciphering his gloom asked, " Where are you going?"

I meant a New branch or something.. He said,

"HOME, retirement aa gaya hai na." A sad contemplative look later he mused, " I live nearby, second house in the lane right next to the Gurudwara. It's an old house. Made it 28 years ago. It is old. But I realised today we are older still."

I had tears in my eyes when I left him working at his temporary desk, trying to bring some semblance of normalcy to his chaotic thoughts. I knew I had been witness to the most personal, deepest gloom an active man feels when he realises his life won't ever be the same again, his routine will change never to be altered again by work. Sure, he'll have time to do things that were left for later when he was busy in his mundane life, making ends meet. He'll travel, spend time with his wife, grandchildren, may be read or write but he'll miss his work. A major part of him will be left behind with his retirement.

May he age well and be happy.

Of God and Other things!

October 8, 2016

I have been an atheist since I understood the concept of God and religion. The idea of bowing and scraping in front of man-made idols always looked ridiculous to me. As a kid, I was made to tag along, when my mother visited religious shrines or temples. Even at that age, I had a weird feeling that people are watching me pray, that they could see right through me and the veneer I put up when I stood in supplication in front of the very idols that made me uncomfortable.

Gradually, when I became old enough to air my opinion, I turned openly agnostic, agreeing to some super power but still not ready to find it in idols and temples. As I grew in confidence, I even started entrusting my friends with the knowledge that their God had never been kind to me. Going as far to say that if He had made us all, He has to tend to all of us irrespective of whether one kneels in prayer or not, that blessed should also be the ones who do not kneel.

Recently, I came across a book on the history of philosophy and religion. An entertaining read at the onset, it soon asked me questions I had never thought about before. Being an avid reader, I have come across books that I stand behind and others that I disagree with. But never in my reading existence, did a book make me feel INSUFFICIENT, like I was missing out on some important piece of the puzzle that would finally complete the giant zigsaw, that life is. It was sheer helplessness to find that I had no faith or any power whatsoever, to put my faith in. It was not just the absence of God but also a total disregard for the bounties I had, things like life, people, comfort, dignity, things that I had always taken for granted, had never thanked anyone for.

I was perturbed. It was like I was in a huge dining room, bustling with activity, every seat taken, people eating, talking, laughing, sharing experiences and suddenly, everybody leaves. The hollowness and ineptitude that I felt, sitting suddenly all alone in that dining hall, was inexplicable. I could still feel the warmth of companionship, hear the tinkle of cutlery, a shadow of laughter here, a shared confidence there.. All gone in a jiffy!

What then, fills that vacuum? What comes inside and never leaves? Cause make no mistake- everything and everyone leaves, sooner or later. Wealth, beloved people, love, friendship and even life. What can, then, help us keep ourselves together? The more I think, the more I believe, it has to be faith.

I spoke to some people I could speak to, about such stuff and a pragmatic atheist friend said-" There is no God. Why do you worry about faith and in whom to put it? You got to have faith in yourself and if you have to put it somewhere put it in your abilities. " Sane advice, granted!! But it didn't stop me thinking and brooding all day long. I have faith in myself, I truly do but that doesn't keep me going when people leave and I am all alone. Gradually, yes, one learns to pick oneself up, dust away the blues and get going again. But even that needs motivation because life does have a way of pulling us down to the rut again and again.

Now, I don't know whether God exists or not, neither can I vouch for any of His miracles but lately something has been tugging at my mind- not religion or spirituality, nothing as lofty as the latter or as superficial as the former. But something deeper, more profound, something I have no words for. A deeper knowledge, may be. A lone thread of self-realization that might lead to consecration and eventual enlightenment and salvation of soul.

A week ago, this would have been impossible to write cause I have always felt that deeper insight into one's psyche is a whole sack of mumbo- jumbo. But I am desperate to have atleast something STAY. Desperation may not be the best motivation to lean towards God but it surely works.

I hope once I find Him, He stays!!!

Just Desserts...

October 11, 2016

Yesterday someone shared an interesting insight about fate, destiny and human behavior with me. She said that our destinies are intertwined with those of the people we meet in our lives. Every acquaintance, friendship or relationship has a purpose in life.

And I agree, people are there so that we learn lessons of life that are otherwise hard to comprehend. Retribution for all our acts is as sure as it is swift. If we hurt someone that is what we get in return, may be not from the same person. If we love someone, all that love is returned, now the catch is that it might not be from the same person as well. Nothing happens without a reason.

We carry so many things on our conscience that without realizing our psyche crumbles under the combined weight of love, life, responsibilities, expectations and reality. We don't even realise what is pulling us down until something inside us snaps and we just have to stop caring about it. Although the weight is off but then again it is a difficult and painful process. It is never easy to let go of something that has become important to you, be it a person, habit, schedule or job, but that is what one has to do to bring a semblance of normalcy to one's chaos.

I envy the pragmatic people, the ones who can keep themselves aloof from all the emotional hiccups and lead a happy life without a care in the world. There is so much to learn from them.

The English idiom about a rolling stone gathering no moss has always had an impact on me. We were taught that it meant that a person who doesn't stay at one place, both geographically and emotionally, doesn't have many ties. I always thought that was a negative attribute. What are we without our worldly ties? What an unfortunate way to live! Don't these people realise that they lose the ones that truly love them when they are busy looking for temporary solace?

But gradually, with time and experience, I realised that the idiom can also mean that stagnation brings rot and those that don't stay attached to a place or people are actually better off. No moss. No excess baggage. More acceptable. Successful. There is so much to learn from rolling stones too.

All said and done, this world is not a wish granting factory, as a famous book says. People eventually get their Just Desserts, some sooner than others. We just have to smile, move on and let our actions decide the course our lives would take.

Being happy is a choice we make. There are some tough decisions involved in the process. Take them. No use wallowing in grief for something that was never meant to be.

The Fall

October 12, 2016

This, right here right now, is the nicest time of the year weather wise. The long grueling summers finally give way to cool breeze and purple skies, a welcome reprieve. Mornings and evenings witness to pinkish cold & people slumber induced. But it is not the cool weather or the purple skies that attract me to these months of pure bliss, it is the trees and the leaves.

There is something magical in the falling of golden leaves. A magic only nature can create. No artist, however proficient, can bring the vivid & vivacious colours of Autumn to his canvas, no writer, however gifted, can ever express the beauty and symbolism of falling leaves in well- strung words, no camera can capture the ethereal quality of nature's bounty in its limited pixels. And I am not even that gifted with words, so I would leave the description of the sublimity of Autumn's splendor to more practiced hands and sharper minds.

I would rather speak about the symbolism of Fall. As in nature, so it is in life. After the harshness of summer months and some tender care of the rainy season, comes a time when the leaves dry up and can no longer hold on to the life giving tentacles of their trees. Nothing changes, per se. The tree stands tall in all its majesty still rooted to its earth but for the leaf it is the end of time, end of a journey which started with it bursting into life, all young and eager.

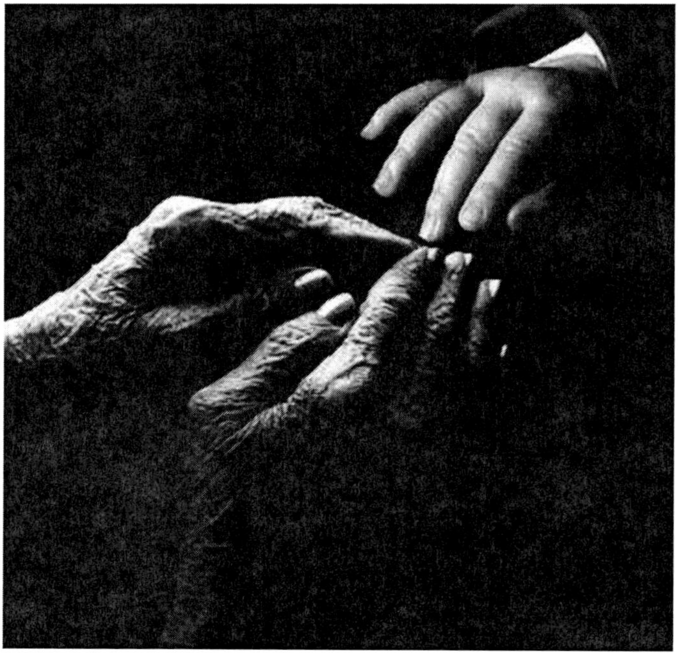

As it grows, it has to endure the tests of time and nature. Come rain or thunderstorms, hail or high water, it stands its ground, fulfilling its life's purpose, funneling vitality into the very tree that holds it. It is torn and drawn and weathered but it still holds on – Fights and wins. And finally when the time approaches, it dessicates shrinking to a wrinkly texture, proud and elegant, connoting a life, well-lived. Its grace does not end with it falling down. Once there, it enriches the soil, thus aiding in the springing up of new life, new leaves.

Such close resemblance to human life. The difference these days is that, people in the autumn of their lives try to pass on the wisdom of their years to often uncomprehending, unheeding, unapologetic youth who always always think that they, themselves, know better.

The human race is sadly missing out on the mysticism and sorcery, that the sagacity of the elderly, can bring about.

Unfortunately, the Autumn of their lives cannot stem the tide of falling values.

Of Hope & Despair...

October 14, 2016

For days now, it has been on my mind. Infact it is the only thing on my mind for the past couple of months. Like other things negative, I thought this too shall pass and probably it would but right now it is getting worse. I know that people who care about me might want to reach out after reading this. I fear that. I really don't want sympathy. That is the reason I was shying away from putting this up on my blog. There might be some people who would find it in bad taste, writing about something so personal and putting it up for the world to read. There might be still others who would think me weak and snively for not being able to hold myself together in the wake of life's challenges. Some would think it a highly pessimistic state of mind despite being so well read. Yet others would feel I am too young to be going through a crisis like that, that it is just a figment of my imagination or something that I have picked up from the various things I read on a daily basis.

However, I, myself, recently got around accepting the fact that it is indeed Depression that I am dealing with. And despite all the misgivings mentioned earlier, I have decided to once and for all write about it and face the consequences later. My decision to write stems from the belief that acceptance is the first step towards healing, gathering courage to share it, is the next.

Such is human psyche that accepting something like this and then trying to talk about it or deal with it, takes a lot of grit & determination. I even wanted to use some other word in lieu of Depression but then that would have been yet another denial, yet another bottling up. The fact that I am writing about it should rule out all kinds of denial.

I don't want to go into the clinical aspects of Depression, they are best left to experts to ponder on. I would only share what I have felt and observed and the ways I would like to be treated by my loved ones.

There is this constant sense of foreboding, of something bad happening. A weight descends on the heart and there is a consistent constriction of the chest. Over-analysing every decision and move becomes a tiring habit and the gravity of expectations, both from self and others, is immense.

Socializing doesn't appeal too much. A feeling of solitude even when surrounded by people, a rote- I am good or I am fine to people's query of How are you?, becomes commonplace. I rather enjoy the company of people I don't know intimately than the ones I do because it eliminates the chances of being asked too many awkward questions. It also helps avoid the possibility of being judged by people on the state of my mind. I hate to be called demented or doddery or stupid or mad or senile.

If someone realises that something is not right, they keep asking me what is wrong and are disappointed when I say that I really don't know. The truth of the matter is that I really don't know what has triggered this or what is feeding it. I don't understand my constant need to cry or being hugged by someone without asking me what the matter is. Eye contact has become a problem, I can't look people in the eye and connect. I lose interest midway in any conversation with anyone.

There are times when I want to confide, some of my surface thoughts, in people I love but can't find words in absence of a strong enough reason for all this. I am also wary of disappointing them in my abilities as a human being of a certain age. It is a societal norm that by this time in my life, I should have everything sorted out, but I don't, so people might judge. Most of all what I dread getting is Sympathy or Pity.

All I want is a little empathy, care, love and an assurance that they'll be there for me in whatever I am going through, no questions asked. I know, no one can change the course of one's life to accommodate the eccentricities of another but isn't that what genuine love and care is all about. If someone is reaching out to you for help, you must be pretty important to them.

I love people who can convey with one hug what a thousand words fail to do- warmth, care, love, strength and a promise that come what may, they will be there, always. Sometimes, it is gratifying to be reassured, in words and deeds, by the ones we love.

All said and done, I feel there is still Hope for me, that I will reach the light at the end of this tunnel, sooner rather than later.

Ethics & the Young

October 18, 2016

Halfway through E. R. Braithwaite's modern classic- To Sir, With Love, I feel a sense of pride to be a part of the teaching community. The patience and perseverance of the protagonist, in dealing with the 'class', is legendary.

I, specifically, feel attached to the scene where 'Sir' decides to take matters in his own hands and let his rowdy, crass class know who was in-charge in his classroom.

The etiquette of language and conduct he lays down for them is as relevant today, if not more. He decides to lead from example. He takes offence on his students using words like 'bleedin', that too used by young adults who come from uneducated, destitute, low on luck families. Compare it to the language used by kids these days and we'd be ashamed of the way our civilization has developed. Children from well to do, educated, cultured backgrounds use words far worse than the innocent looking 'bleedin' and feel cool doing so.

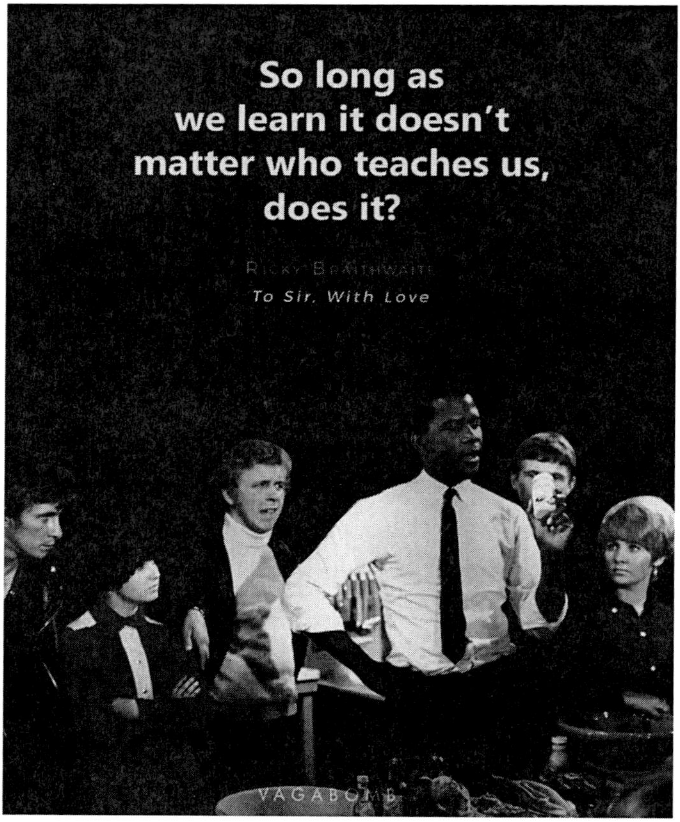

The respect he suggests, they accord each other by addressing the girls with Miss and boys by surname, is also a lost art these days. I have been a teacher too long to know that students these days don't even extend this courtesy to their teachers and elders.

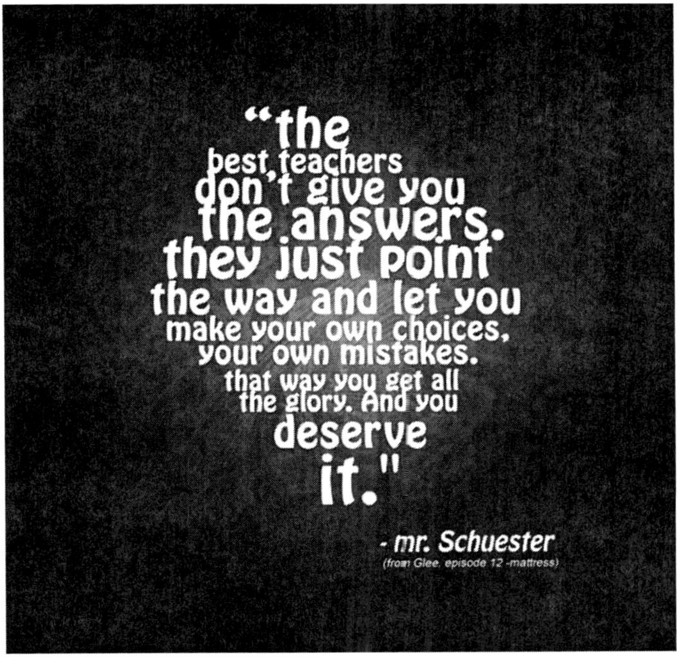

Not long ago, we were students too and we looked up to our teachers, treated them with a deference befitting their station as bestowers of knowledge and wisdom. I hate to generalize, but this attribute is largely missing from students today.

Just a few days back, I was talking to someone about a whole different thing and I told him that it is only the first time something happens that we don't approve of or like, that we are disappointed. Beyond that first time, it is expected behavior. We may not like it but we, then, don't expect conformity. Same stands true for inculcating the virtues of good language, sound conduct and etiquette amongst a class full of students who are bent on believing that their cool quotient is more important than boring adherence to manners. Initial disappointment gives way to expectations of obnoxious behavior.

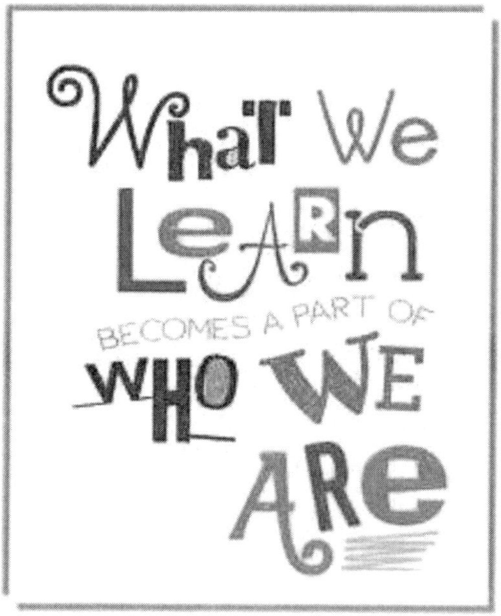

That said, I still believe that taking the advice of one's elders and teachers stand people in good stead in the long run. The morals passed on through the generations is pure gold. The values, thus imparted and absorbed, stand the tests of time.

Every generation has its fill of uncouth & boorish students with indecorous and bawdy behavior, it is left to the teaching community, more than anyone, to bring them to grade, to polish them into shining examples of human decency. Even if a handful of our charges from a class, take our teachings to heart and turn into compassionate, responsible and well-mannered adults, our work is accomplished.

There will always be a few who fail us in our attempts to breed decorum and instill virtuous, winsome traits in their character but that is a personal choice not a teacher's shortcoming. We need to rise above that and keep up our diligent efforts in pursuit of our noble profession.

Down Memory Lane

October 19, 2016

Remembrance, Reminiscence, Recollection or simply memory- a thing or feeling that stays even after it is long gone. Sometimes such retrospective moments are so strong and vivid that one has no choice but to leave the present in order to delve into these cherished flashbacks-these seldom visible permanent residents of our mind.

I have been ill for the past few days now and my ailment warrants a lot of massaging of my limbs, a task that inevitably falls on mom. She has such a pleasant bedside manner. To take my mind off the pain she keeps talking of more pleasant things and that's how we got talking of my childhood today. Since our childhood, my father's mantra for us has been-family first. And I live by it. But, in the course of our lives we chance upon many people and relationships that become inalienable parts of us. My write up today, talks about some of these select few.

Today mom so fondly recalled my mischievous streak as a child, that I was transported back to those happier times when things were so easy, so uncomplicated. We lived on the first floor of a double story rented house. The ground floor was occupied by an extremely affectionate punjabi family. I was reminded of the lady of that house today. A small, dainty, loving woman whom my sisters and I called Mumma. She had three children of her own, all grown up and disciplined but the kind of love she reserved for us was exceptional. I remember running down the stairs to hide behind her everytime I did something that ordained a scolding or punishment from mom. When quite young, I used to avoid oral medication of any sort. When given capsules or tablets to swallow, I used to throw them down the drain. One day, mom found out. I was given the whacking of my life, I bawled like a street urchin and it was Mumma who came running to save me from further lacing. It was her, I used to run to when the compounder came home to give me a flu shot or something like that. She was our favorite hiding place.

She passed on, a few years back but her memories that enriched our childhood will always remain fresh in my heart.

While on nostalgia mode, I got thinking about the great times I had with my friends. The 'garam chais' and bread maska we went out for, while teaching at Mody School. The long days and equally grueling evenings spent working at my desk but with so much fun. I remember friends, some of whom still are in touch, others who have moved on geographically and emotionally. The unsuppressed, unaffected laughter, the mindless chatter, sincerely discussing things as mundane as they were irrelevant. Yes, friends are important. There are just a few, but all of them find a special warm corner in my heart.

While on special relationships, I also thought of two people so close to my heart that I can barely breathe for the love and care I carry for them. My heart is overwhelmed with tenderness at the mere thought or mention of any one of them. Those two are the children I never had. Though I haven't had the privilege of knowing them since their births and the time spent with them has been limited, at most but the bond is permanent, irreplaceable, irreversible and irrevocable. Fond memories of times spent with her and the long chats with him will always stay in my heart wherever they choose to go or even when life takes them away from me on a journey of their own, which will ineluctably happen.

I had all the time in the world lying in bed for a couple of days and thoughts of days gone by kept intruding- some funny, some hurtful, others happy or sad. But that is life!! It wouldn't be completely fulfilling if there was only the hue of happiness to color our canvases with.

I am so deeply entrenched in memories today, thinking of people and events, places and friends, children & their choices, that I just wish I could go back in time to my happy carefree days or hold on to the ones I can still have.

Beyond my wishes, the only tangible things I have are these Memories.

Love's illusions I recall

October 21, 2016

I am not a huge fan of pop music from the 50s and the 60s. The first time I heard this beautiful song was in the movie Love Actually, some 9 years back. And, about four years after that a very dear student gave me this song to listen. Since then, Joni Mitchell's version of this masterpiece has always remained on my playlist and I have delighted in its cadence thousands of times. I have always admired the raspy timbre of her voice. The gruff, scratchy sound goes perfectly well with the cover of the album, with her holding a cigarette in one hand and a glass of red wine lying in wait.

It is only recently that I got to know that Frank Sinatra, considered by music enthusiasts as one of the most iconic & influential 20th century artists, also rendered his voice to a version of the same song during his reprise years. Although his voice is timeless but I would still go with Joni Mitchell's version any given day.

The sublimity of this song lies not only in her rendition but also the soul stirring lyrics. It's the words that resonate with me every time I listen to this song. I have posted the lyrics in hope that the readers may marvel at the exalting text.

Rows and flows of angel hair
And ice cream castles in the air
And feather canyons everywhere
I've looked at clouds that way
But now they only block the sun
They rain and snow on everyone
So many things I would have done
But clouds got in my way
I've looked at clouds from both sides now
From up and down, and still somehow
It's cloud illusions I recall
I really don't know clouds at all
Moons and Junes and Ferris wheels
The dizzy dancing way you feel
As every fairy tale comes real

I've looked at love that way
But now it's just another show
You leave 'em laughing when you go
And if you care, don't let them know
Don't give yourself away
I've looked at love from both sides now
From give and take, and still somehow
It's love's illusions I recall
I really don't know love at all
Tears and fears and feeling proud
To say "I love you" right out loud
Dreams and schemes and circus crowds
I've looked at life that way
But now old friends are acting strange
They shake their heads, they say I've changed
Well something's lost, but something's gained
In living every day
I've looked at life from both sides now
From win and lose and still somehow
It's life's illusions I recall
I really don't know life at all

There are quite a few songs that can make the list if I start writing about them but my purpose today is to convey a message of love and hope to a very dear, affectionate person who needs it today. I am sure he will peruse this write up as he always does with my blogs. I think he'll recognize the song and appreciate why I chose it, in the first place.

To him I want to say- Whatever trials and confusion you are going through are temporary. It is just a phase. Love and life are illusions to most people even if they gain intimate knowledge of them. No one can claim to understand them completely. There is no fixed recipe for happiness. Not all our desires are fulfilled. That said, we still live our lives and find happiness in whatever blessings we already have. I hope you find peace and happiness too.

May you come back stronger and better.

I've looked at life from both sides now

From up and down and still somehow

It's life's illusions I recall

I really don't know life at all

I Believe in Magic

October 22, 2016

"Do you like Country music?" asked Prakirti. My last blog must have led her to believe that I understood the western music scene quite well, so I told her that my musical education was sporadic, at best. And that it was quite late in life that I had picked up English songs and artists. Hence, differentiating genres was beyond me. She said, "Let me send you a selection of songs, then." She did. And I instantly fell in love with this beauty.

Don Williams – I Believe in You

I don't believe in superstars

Organic food and foreign cars

I don't believe the price of gold

The certainty of growing old
That right is right and left is wrong
That north and south can't get along
That east is east and west is west
And bein' first is always best.
Well, I dont believe that heaven waits
For only those who congregate
I'd like to think of God as love
He's down below
He's up above
He's watchin' people everywhere
He knows who does and doesn't care
And I'm an ordinary man
Sometimes I wonder who I am.
I know with all my certainty
What's goin' on with you and me
Is a good thing
It's true
I believe in you.
I dont believe virginity
Is as common as it used be
In workin' days and sleepin' nights
That black is black and white is white
That Superman and Robinhood
Are still alive in Hollywood
That gasoline's in short supply

The risin' cost of gettin' by
I believe in love
I believe in babies
I believe in mom and dad
And I believe in you.

Once again, I was done in by the soothing music, the bewitching and entrancing strains of the guitar, the charismatic baritone of Don Williams and most of all by the lyrics – Words, weaving Magic. So simple yet of such import.

Out of all the delightful things that the artist says, he believes in, I chose MAGIC as the title of my blog. I shall try and elucidate, rather justify my choice of title in my plain, ingenuous expression.

The writers of the song and the artist who made it so popular might have concentrated on Love, I like Magic. For me love is magic, faith is magic, music is magic, divine providence is magic, mom-dad-babies-children-old folk all Magic.

Not even a week has gone by, I was down and out, suffering from despair. I wrote about it. Magic transpired. I got support from unexpected quarters. People who were long gone, without any contact whatsoever, reached out. Mere acquaintances came forward with their stories, experiences and suggestions. I was pulled out of the dark by so many helping hands. I received calls from people I had never spoken to and they made small talk feel so relieving (case in point, Prakirti, the child who gave me this song and set the ball rolling for this piece here.. Thank you. Grateful!) I was so happy to find so much love & care that indifference & 'what can I say to this' attitude from the people I expected relief from, also did not dampen my spirit. I had embraced Hope. Pure Magic. Bliss.

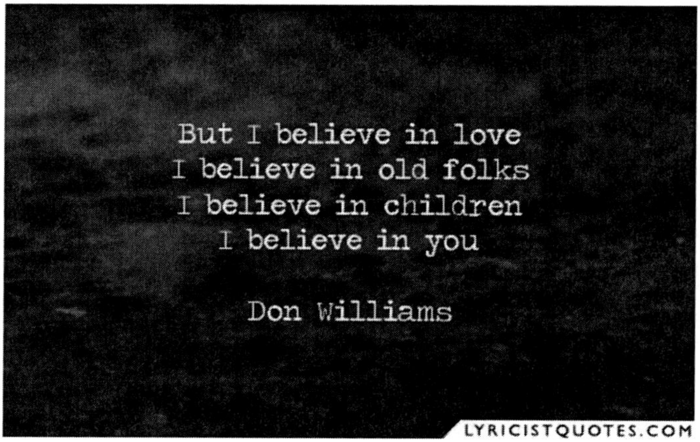

I have often heard people say- Do not be afraid. Go ahead, do your part and things will automatically fall into place. I feel a certain amount of fear of the unknown, of the outcome, of the process is a great motivator in getting things done. Fear is magic too. Just the right amount and you are on your way.

The most splendid, resplendent, glorious of all Magic is the ability to connect with People. Family-parents, grandparents, siblings, sons, daughters, cousins, friends, co-workers, colleagues or even for that matter the strangers we come across everyday while walking down a street or entering a building, attending a concert or a show, shopping in a mall or arcade. People are everywhere. Just smiling down at them creates Enchantment– a mystic energy that envelops us and makes us believe in each other. It coerces, compels & drives us to be more accepting of our differences, of each other's opinions & circumstances. Acceptance is Magic. Belief in each other is Magic.

I believe in Magic✨. I believe in You-my people💖, my circle of light 💫, my ring of faith.😇

Deconstructing (the) Diwali Dilemma

October 25, 2016

No, my dilemma this festive season does not root from the confusion of whether or not I should light India made Diyas or Chinese bulbs , or whether I should have a Diwali with or without firecrackers. Not for me, this moral or political high ground! My predicament is more mundane and it has a peculiar character & tendency of visiting me every year, without fail. The only thing I concern myself with on this festive season year after year is whether To Clean Or Not to Clean.

Yes, my plight deals with the annual Diwali Safai, an integral part of the pre-festival preparations. No Indian household can afford to take this schedule lightly because is it not the clean, freshly painted houses that attract Goddess Laxmi, the diety of wealth and prosperity?

I, vividly, remember being made to clean all the dabbas from mom's kitchen every year when I was a kid. Unsuspecting, as all kids are at that age, we rather enjoyed this exercise as at the end of it we were rewarded with little bric-a-brac from the kitchen which could then be used by us when we played house (all girls did that😅). The annual de-cluttering relieved mom of things accumulated over the years which surprisingly were important once and funnily enough received such step motherly treatment when she threw them out. I have lost count of the times I heard her say, "When did I buy this and for heaven's sake, why?"

Now that some considerable years have passed, the responsibility of maintaining the house and carrying forward the grandiose Diwali tradition of Safai has fallen on us. The vein in which I started this write up makes it evidently clear that I am not too keen on picking up a broom and cleaning away to glory. In fact, I would do anything to avoid the eventuality of visiting the oft-left alone, corners of the house.

My younger sister, on the other hand, takes after my mother and is brimming with ideas of how to, what to and when to clean. What to throw out and what to keep is next on her agenda. The atmosphere around the house is one of general de-worming, people who have pets or love them will understand the analogy- a necessary evil, in my opinion. Wiping, scouring, scrubbing, uncluttering, it seems is cathartic to her. It would have been solid gold, if she did not feel the urge to involve each of us in her party. She has specific, carefully scripted instructions for all of us and dare we go awry. She is a hard task master, my sister.

Anyhow, I am, most of the time, spared the more gritty and onerous tasks because I have a deep set allergy to Dust. Speaking metaphorically about unpalatable & unpleasant things in life, a very close friend had once told me that such things have to be approached in a meticulous manner, just like one would deal with allergies. He said, and I quote-

1st. You prepare yourself mentally that the thing which you are allergic to won't affect you. I mean you need to make it sure in your head, a mental resolve of sorts.

2nd. You need to start taking little doses of that thing on a routine basis. No need to increase the dose.

3rd. In some time, you will note that it has stopped bothering you and the allergy is effectively gone.

Now, I agree that it is a methodical approach to life and may work well for some pragmatic people, specially in life situations (he goes about and accosts all his life decisions, big or small, in this clinical and highly unemotional fashion)

But, it may not work for the likes of yours truly. You see, commendable as this idea is, I would still rather like to laze around on account of my allergy than to win it over and become a slave to my sister's tyrannical Safai instructions every Diwali.

Now that most of the pre-diwali cleaning is over, we can all heave a collective sigh of relief at home and get on with the shopping and celebration part of the festival. May this Diwali be safe and bring a lot of peace, tranquility, happiness and prosperity for everyone reading this blog.

I have to be looking around for an apt gift for my dear sister after what I have done to her in this write up. She knows, though, that she makes all our lives beautiful, lights them up, just by being here.

The Final Frontier

October 31, 2016

Diwali festivities over, I had a wonderful day today with guests and relatives, friends and loved ones turning up to meet us. Yet another gentle reminder that life is worth living and celebrating only when you have your people around to share it with you and rejoice in it.

The day started going downhill when I had this weird feeling of loss and emotional emptiness after we had all turned in for the night. While going through my Facebook timeline, I came across a dedication , a condolence message from one of my friends in memory of one of his.

I had tears in my eyes at the sheer helplessness & ineptitude of man when faced with fate. The young, handsome face of that unknown individual shook me to the core. Dedications ranged from calling him a hearty, jovial, ambitious, full of life person to his keen interest in photography and a general zest for life. Some of his friends had mentioned how he refused to get married before he made something of his life, how he wanted to become someone for his family- his parents before he embarked on a journey of marital bliss. He wanted to make them proud.

To be taken away so cruelly in an accident on a day when most of us were celebrating the festival of lights, left everyone of his friends speechless. All the posts dedicated to him, tagging him carried his smiling, dashing pictures and all of them invariably wanted him back because so much was left unsaid, unspoken, unfinished... I was moved beyond belief. Tears came unbidden.

We take so much for granted. We forget that this life we have is so uncertain. Just like Navdeep, we may be celebrating one moment, devouring ladoos, and be gone the next, leaving dazed family members and loved ones to pick up the pieces of shattered lives, dashed hopes and unfulfilled dreams. There is just so much riding on us, we fail to notice.

We do not acknowledge that the final frontier may come to us sooner than we expect. Instead we while away our lives fighting with our loved ones, keeping grudges, leaving things unsaid, loving people and not letting them know. We think we have all the time in the world but we don't.

When we recognize that we don't have all the time in the world, we see our priorities most clearly.

~ Laura Carstensen

Word Porn

We need to re-prioritize our lives. Know what is important, acknowledge the people who are there for us- no matter what, stop fighting, shelf our egos, love without restraint, be thankful, commit to life & people and stop hurting the ones who have been there and who promise to stay. Believe me, nothing is more important than earning love and respect in your lifetime. After all, it is meaningless if people just praise you when you are gone. It is the difference you make in lives, while you are still alive and kicking, that counts.

You can't do anything about the length of your life, but you can do something about its width and depth.

- H. L. Mencken

Word Porn

It may be a naive attempt at writing but my message is clear. Apologise if you are wrong, help if you can, try to understand the perception of others, be tolerant. save relationships, say it if you care, quit hurting people & be grateful for all that you have. Making money is important but at the end of the day, it isn't everything. Judge what brings you happiness, true heartfelt pleasure. Is it the idea of being rich, of finding solace in temporary people or things, of validation from your peers or is it being blessed with people who love you, who are permanent in life, that brings true richness and meaning to your ordinary existence?

Think and act now because what we can't achieve before death knocks us down, remains as regret in one heart or the other. Choose well what you wish your life to be.

Unshackling the Mind.

November 14, 2016

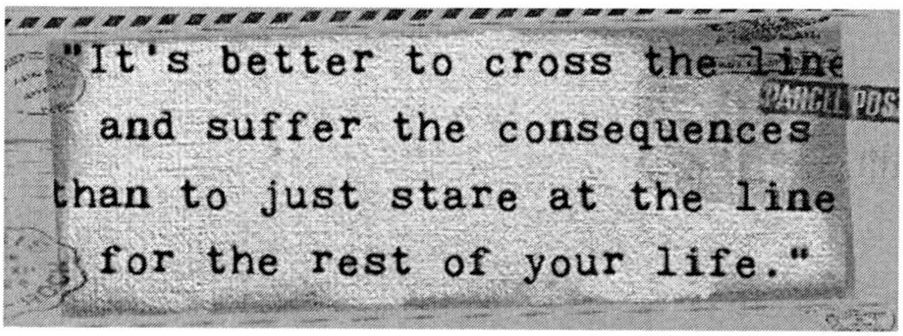

Not for everyone, Small Town Living.

Not for everyone, the Fetters of Conservatism.

Not for everyone, the Maxims of Society.

Not for everyone, the Inhibitions of Gender.

If you happen to dwell in small town India, you would agree that lives here are lived more out of duty & honor of the family rather than for Self. Nothing wrong with keeping family first or adhering to the norms laid by them but it cannot be the end all and be all for an individual. We were born as an individual soul and it is our foremost duty to make sure that our soul is growing , that it is happy and healthy. Unfortunately, inevitably, we succumb to the wishes and diktats of the family or society and largely curb the small indulgences that our Self seeks.

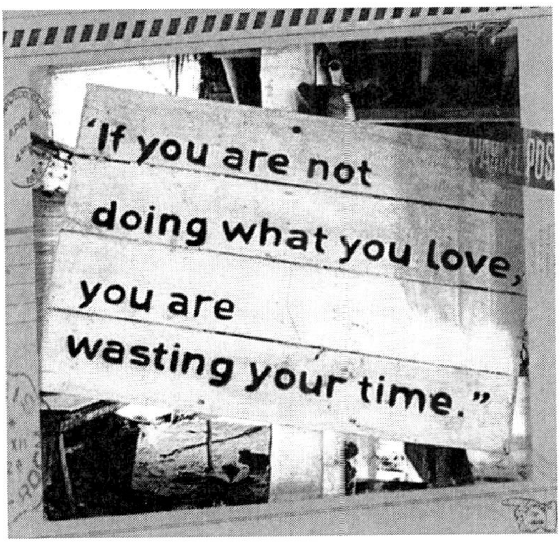

We may find comfort & fulfillment in travel, books, connecting with people, writing, music, love, friendship- all of which are designed as choices an individual can make. But as engulfed in the guidelines of age old conservatism as we are, we unavoidably think – what would people think if we make any of the above individual choices. Will we be acceptable to the society? What will our parents feel? Is going against the tide worth all that dissension? Are we the only people around, who are compromising on our dreams and happiness? If others can give up on small pleasures of the soul like these, why can't we conform too? Are girls even supposed to think so freely? Do girls not owe it to their parents to abide by the code laid down for their own safety and virtue?

We forget that this life here, that we have been endowed with, is precious. We cannot and should not go through it denying ourselves gratification in order to appease others. People have different sets of rules for themselves and for others. Whatever we might do, not everyone would be happy. So why not make the Self happy? No one is squeaky clean. A close friend recently explained to me the fact that, the cleaner people look the more dirt they've swept under the rug. Why, then, should we pay any heed to their counsel and deny ourselves lifestyle choices that may lead to satisfaction and delight for Self?

Take that trip that you have been yearning for, read-write-create if that is your poison, sing-play-enjoy any music that ups your spirit, opt for a job that gives wings to your imagination-something that inspires you to get up every morning and go to work, meet people, make friends, fall in love. Never apologise for the choices you make. Let go of the constant conscience pangs and guilt trips. We are not here to please others. We are here to live our lives as best as we can. Yes, we are responsible to the people who love us or those we love- our parents, children, friends, spouses. But none of them is entitled to use that love as a leash to keep us chained & bolted. The biggest debt we owe is to ourselves.

What is the worst that can happen if we follow our hearts? We may not succeed at a job or in a relationship but atleast we would have the satisfaction of having tried. We gave ourselves a chance to be what we envisioned. There will be lessons along the way but good or bad, they will be the ones we are ready for, because they would be in direct consequence of the path we took of our own volition. We would learn to gather our pieces and move forward instead of trying to place the blame on the very people whose love tethers us to an unremarkable routine life.

It all starts with the Mind. If we can train our minds to let go of the guilt that our choices ineluctably bring, then, gradually, we will be successful in Unshackling the ties that bind us to the mundane. We can, then, prevail and give meaning to our tales. We are not born to breathe, adapt and die. We are all stories in the making. Let's put our hearts into the making of our very own blockbuster.

✨Coup de Grace!!!✨

December 29, 2016

I hope that someday
when I am gone,
someone,
somewhere,
picks my soul up
off of these pages
and thinks,
"I would have loved her."

Nicole Lyons

Word Porn

I choose to love you in silence
For in silence, I find no rejection.
I choose to love you in loneliness
For in loneliness, no one owns you but me.
I choose to adore you from a distance
For distance will shield me from pain.
I choose to hold you in my dreams
For in my dreams, you have no end.
-Jalaluddin Rumi

Endings are always painful & difficult. Be it anything. Any relationship, habit, time, custom, tradition, thing or trend that ends has once been a living, thriving part of our life, growth or routine. A definitive conclusion or how things play out is, thus, a significant part of our lives and needs to be written about.

It would be the most logical assumption that the end of another year has brought about such ruminative notions to the fore. In a way it is correct. One tends to sit and contemplate on the year gone by and the trials and triumphs that it brought along in its wake. Yet again, year ends are neither times to lament nor celebrate, as a year is just Time, it is constant, eternal. Time doesn't end. It is just our reactions to the situations it presents that constitute the very framework of our being.

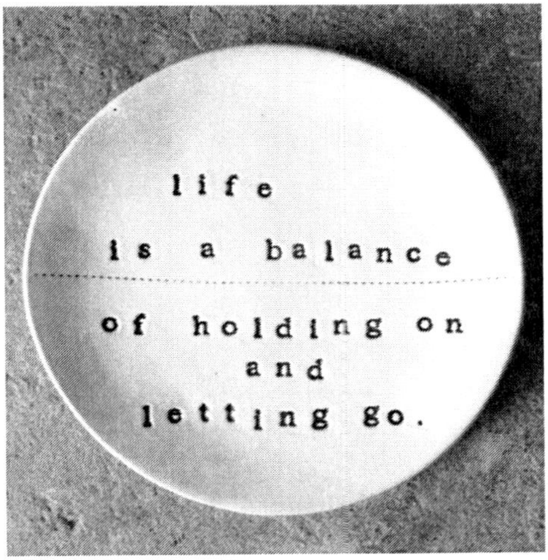

There were so many different thoughts running about in my mind for this year-end blog that a few weeks back I did something I had never done before. I jotted down some notes with the intent of using them for channelizing my erratic ideas into a fairly coherent piece of writing. But some things are just not meant to be. I just couldn't piece them together into a write up. I have always written spontaneously. Planned writing has never been my forte. I write, in the moment.

I am a firm believer in the power of grey. In my humble opinion, nothing is always ever completely white or black. Our lives cannot be classified or arranged in clear spaces or brackets of right or wrong, loss or gain, happiness or pain. Such gradation is just not justified. Yet so fickle is the human mind that we tend to forget the happy moments and concentrate on the losses.

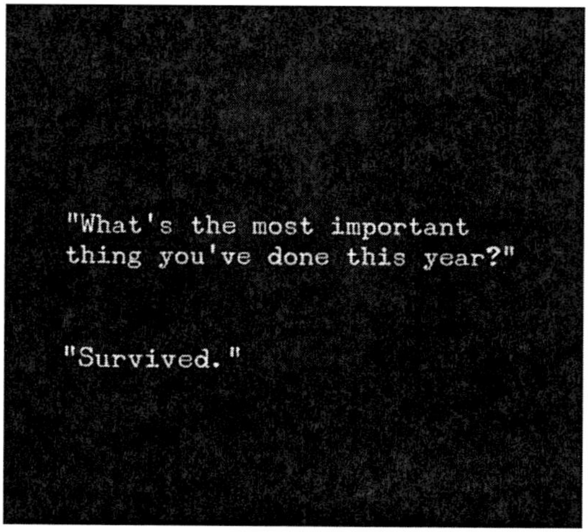

The biggest loss that I had to endure this year was the parting of ways with an important person in my life. It was hard giving up on a relationship that I had come to value more than most. Never before had I fought so hard to retain someone in my life but then, never before had anyone called me Maa and gifted me with an overwhelming feeling of immense love and fulfillment while it lasted. His life choices took him away from me. We drifted apart before it became too ugly for him. But, love still remains. I hope & pray that his choice brings him love, peace & happiness and that the ensuing years guide him to the path of contentment and success. Although he has been a regular, inseparable part of my life and writings for the past many years, this is the last time he will find reference in my blogs because I am of the resolute opinion that if one cannot stay & if it has to be distant, it better not be. No use flogging a dead horse or watering a dead plant, the language is replete with metaphors.

This year, I witnessed some of my very close friends and acquaintances suffering irreparable losses at the hands of fate, destiny, Providence. The void that such a bereavement or misfortune leaves, is hard to be replenished by anything this world has to offer. No words of solace, acts of kindness or passing of time can completely heal the hurt. Yes, with time people get used to living in a certain way because this is life and if nothing else, it is never short on distractions. Yet the emptiness and gaping wounds cannot be palliated by any prescription. Even then, as they say, life is for the living and one has to move on and keep on living for the people who are and who care. None of us has the luxury to sit back and nurse our broken hearts and spirits. There is life to be lived, responsibilities to be carried out and people to be loved & supported. I hope & pray that the coming years give them reasons to rejoice, sooner rather than later- reasons that have the subtlety to soothe these troubled and shattered souls.

Recently, I had occasion to visit my native place and spend some days with my extended family. I always believed that life in the countryside is much simpler, relationships more pure and innocent than their counterparts in the cities. The rustic grandeur of stone paved pathways and dusty lanes crammed with cattle & livestock along with playing, laughing, screaming children held a special attraction for me. The sights, sounds, smells of the rural kind never ceased to amaze me. Their lifestyle, their food and the thought they put into each relationship by dint of being always in each others' touch, drew me magnetically towards them. Many of these rosy-eyed beliefs of mine were in for a rude shock when I got a chance to spend some time with the rural folk. My mind initially refused to register the terrible intrigues & internal feuds, the constant back-stabbing & back- biting, the ubiquitous plotting & scheming of sub-urban people. It was worse than the neglect most city people come across at the hands of their fellow city-dwellers, on a daily basis because it wasn't expected in a close knit community spread a little over three kilometers. The degeneration of morals and family values opened my eyes to new vistas of country life. My trust in the concept of family, filial & community obligations and the significance of kith & kin, that my father has brought me up with, was shaken to its very core. To say that the visit was a disappointment is an understatement of giant proportions. It was downright vulgar to behold such deterioration of human character in our own backyard. I hope & pray that in the year ahead, people, there, would realize the flaws, fallacy, laxity & errors of their ways and work towards restoring the bucolic charm of the village.

This year, I was a silent onlooker of the changes my sisters brought about in their lives. I saw my younger sister fight her inner demons and come out victorious at the end. I witnessed her transformation from a broken, tottering person to a strong, self-assured, assertive individual who doesn't pay heed to the censure of society. Societal norms and age-old patriarchal maxims don't govern her life and decisions. No one, but she, regulates what is right or wrong for her and her child. I salute her tenacity in the face of adversity. I, also, greatly admire the never-say-die attitude of my elder sister. She dared to brave and confront life at its lowest and ventured into areas she had never dreamt she would have to go into, with extreme patience and grace. I hope & pray the coming years be kind to them and theirs. I pray for more strength, perseverance, tolerance and courage for these two indomitable, indefatigable and earnest women.

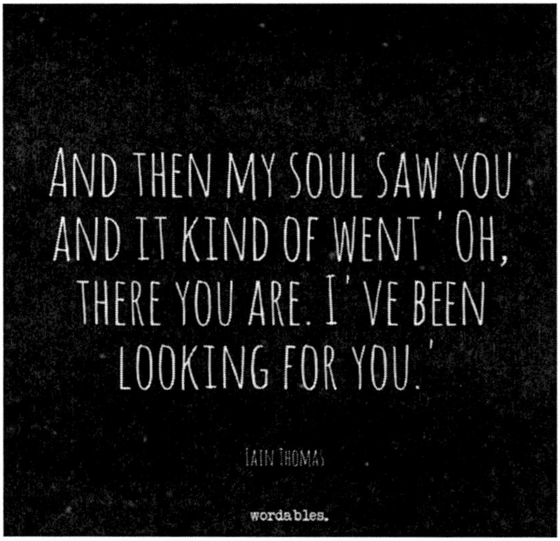

Last but not the least, a special mention needs to be made of two people who don't want to be cited in any of my write-ups and yet read them all, word by word. I know the written word doesn't mean much to you. You are both assured & confident of the bond we share and yet here I am, being grateful to God that I got to know you better and that we have had such good years together. I am much obliged by the love and constant care you accord me. It is, indeed, a privilege knowing you. I hope & pray that you, my confidantes, receive all that you seek in life and that the next year or the years ahead would never leave you wanting in any aspect of your existence.

✨Happy New Year to all readers!! ✨

Auld Lang Syne

A Tribute...
By Sujata Bhatt

January 8, 2017

Grief is such a personal emotion and yet reminiscing someone we love after they have passed on, through our words or in our hearts, is cathartic, therapeutic even. November last year, my friend, philosopher & guide- Sujata di, lost her mother. The raw pain and grief I witnessed, when I went to offer my condolences, was heartbreaking. She, at last, found it in herself to write about Aunty. What I share below is her tribute to the extraordinary woman that her Ma was. When I asked di whether I could share it on my blog, she just said, "You may, if you feel it is alright. I want people to know her." I had the good fortune of having met her and I wish I had known her better. Rest in peace Aunty!

Farewell, Ma….

Driving alone to Lucknow on a

Sunday evening, I saw my mother
in my mind's eye, smile,
and beckon me into
her arms, gathering me close to
her heart and I realized
that the warmth of her
love was the
most precious thing I had in my life,
but on reaching home, this image
dissolved to reveal
the shocking truth...
under the oxygen mask, my
mother struggled to breathe,
her frail, bird-like frame
rapidly sinking under...
and as I held desperately, fiercely
on to her hands, she bid me goodbye, her
eyes finding mine, then slowly
becoming still...
Her final journey had begun
and
I sobbed, 'Rest in peace, Ma',

all I did was cry and cry and cry...

(2nd Dec, 2016)

(With apologies to Kamla Das)

MA

My All and all!

(22nd May, 1936 to 15th Nov., 2016)

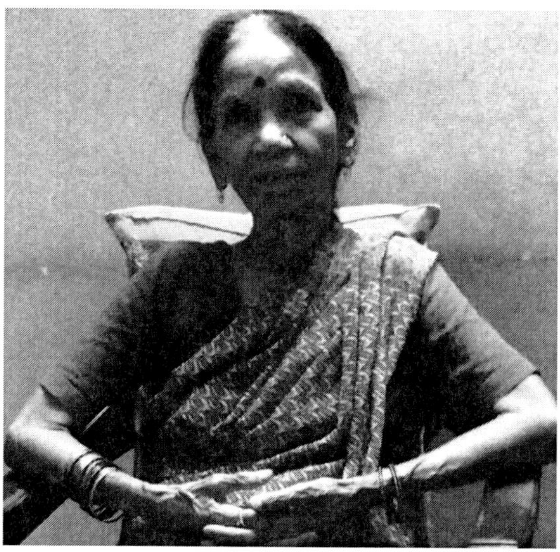

I don't remember being born or being gathered to Ma's bosom as an infant, but I remember the love and warmth that emanated from her all my life...........

I don't remember the pain of the umbilical cord being severed between us, but I remember the powerful bond that tied me to her till the very end.....and beyond.

I don't remember the early years of my growing-up. I get a glimpse of them through the sepia-tinted photos that I flick through occasionally: here, she cuddles me to her heart, feeding me something; there, I stand with a comb in my hand as she looks at me lovingly; in one, I'm a toddler, not yet having learnt to walk, being held by each hand, by Papa and Ma; in so many of them, I'm hardly recognizable with Ma having dolled me up in lehnga and dupatta, or a hat and a stylishly stitched frock or the one where, as a three-year old, I sit within the protective circle of my parents. So many moments that I have no recollection of, but when I look back over the course of thirty years or so, make me realize none of that love and care and warmth had abated or tapered off. It burned as fiercely as ever-in the way she looked at me, smiled at me or sat by me.

As long as I can remember, I have turned to Ma for advice, for support, for answers and I've always been given what I asked for and more. She seemed to know just the right things to say and the most suitable ways to do them. Unconsciously, I tried to copy her in all that she did. I didn't even know I had a fetish for cleanliness and order until I realized, I had watched her meticulous way of keeping house; in the words of The Police "every little thing she did was magic".

It has just hit me that she was no ordinary mortal; well, she didn't move mountains or bring about revolutions, but there was something about her that set her apart from everyone I knew. She was utterly and completely without artifice. She would call a spade a spade, no matter how we felt about it; at times, her forthrightness would embarrass us among friends and relatives and we would grin weakly to dissipate the ensuing awkwardness. In really delicate situations, we actually coached her to be a trifle diplomatic and not say what was uppermost in her mind, but it was always a losing battle. Ma could not gloss over an unpleasantness and more often than not, the person who had rubbed her the wrong way would have to bear the brunt of her displeasure, come what may. It wasn't deliberate, it was just who she was. There are very few people who were irksome to her, but her very demeanor in their presence, would become so unapproachable and disapproving, that they invariably sensed it and refrained from annoying her further. Tact in Ma, was a rarity, indeed!

Ma was devoid of all the vices that plague us at some point of our lives. I know it sounds like an impossibility, but the Creator had done a marvellous job in putting her together in flesh and blood. Her honesty, her lack of avarice, her principles and her strong moral values made her an exceptional human being. There was a purity about her that made me more fully aware of my own shortcomings. In her presence, you were forced to face your own weaknesses and find ways to overcome them. Each one of us accepts this amazing quality that Ma possessed. Her simplicity was so genuine, it shone right out of her. She made me feel humble. I wish I'd bowed before her or touched her feet or placed rose-petals on them to show her what I felt for her in a more tangible way. Instead, it was all very tacit. I own today, that I have revered and adored and worshipped no one else my entire life, as I have Ma; I just wish I could've told her that when there had been time.....

There had always, been a mystery surrounding Ma and Papa's marriage. Ma never gave us the whole story. It was from bits and pieces gleaned from Saroj mausi, Mukul mausi and Ma herself, that I could piece this mesmerizing saga of love, sacrifice and banishment together. Apparently, Ma discovered that she had special feelings for Papa at the tender age of 17 or 18. A motherless waif, she established herself as a wonderful cook in a tiny kitchen, where she prepared savories to feed a horde of siblings and cousins, though hardly ever had any left to feed herself. Papa was a regular visitor to the household and was studying under the patronage of Bade Nana, the family patriarch. Papa was thin as a rake in those days (I can vouch for this fact, courtesy pictures of the time) and I'd often teased Ma as to what had attracted her to him! She would always be very serious about it and told us it was not always the appearance of a person that mattered. In a large family, comprising of sisters, brothers, cousins and sisters in-law, it was easy to overlook the quieter members who chose to remain in the shadows. Papa's attention and care for Ma must have gravitated her to him and when the two decided to marry, it shouldn't have come as a surprise. But it did!

The announcement sent shock waves through the residents of the stone and cement edifice that was 30, Kutchehry Road.

The Srivastava clan was an influential one in Lucknow. Bade Nana was a stalwart and moved in rarefied society; a renowned lawyer, who had traveled to London and owned, one of the very few Chevrolet Convertibles in the city, his word, both actually and figuratively, was the law! He refused permission, absolutely; no such match would take place under his jurisdiction. Papa was adamant, too. I believe, he even exhorted Ma to elope. But Ma was Ma. That went against all the scruples she held sacred. Eventually, Ma's maternal uncle took it upon himself to solemnize the union. Hasty arrangements were made in Faizabad, where Nana was a District Cane Development Officer. The 'baraat' was a ragtag group of Papa's few friends and my sole Chacha, constituting the bridegroom's family, other than the groom himself! To their credit, Chhote Nana and all Ma's siblings attended the Arya Samaj ceremony that saw Km. Malti Srivastave become Mrs. Malti Bhatt. There were muted grumblings in the family against Papa for carrying away the sweetest girl of the household, a grudge that was nurtured and continued for fifteen long years. Ma and Papa left Lucknow for Rourkela and thereon to Ranchi and did not come back to the city until Deepa Mausi's wedding in 1978. Ma was not invited to Kishan Mama, Umesh Mama, Bishnu Mama or Chitra Mausi's weddings. Forsaken and forgotten, I can only imagine how desolate and abandoned she must have felt, treated this way by her own kith and kin. In spite of my urging, Ma never spoke about her early years of married life. She did suffer a miscarriage though, before me, and Mohini Mami had come down to Ranchi to take care of her. Nana wouldn't have been able to keep up the pretence of anger and disapproval against this eldest daughter, I feel.

Though my memories of Ma in the late 60s are hazy, I do recall her as a slim, graceful, woman who loved to do everything to perfection. For her, neatness and orderliness were bywords. She couldn't imagine being in a house where these were absent. I remember often riffling through her dressing table drawers, finding a 'jooda' and 'jooda' pins and asking her what they were for; I'd never seen her use them! I vaguely remember her long hair, reaching below her waist, which she always kept in a loose braid. Ma's beauty was very subtle. Her simplicity defined it and perhaps, accentuated it. When she was getting ready to go somewhere, I would sit on the dressing table and watch intensely as she applied a straight 'bindi' out of a liquid phial on her wide forehead, the Angel Face compact which she'd used forever (until production of it was stopped), homemade 'kajal', with a slight slant outwards, which gave a beautiful serenity to her eyes and the saree, that she draped to precision, with nary a pleat out of place. When Ma slipped into her sandals, I wanted to applaud -"My mummy, bestest!"

I also wish to note another marvel about Ma. Even when the temperatures hit the high 40s, she never broke into a sweat. There was no body odor—none–that came off her. She exuded either a whiff of Pond's Dream flower Talc or her much loved Charlie. Mala Bhabhi always used to bring her a bottle on her visits from the US. (It is a cruel turn of fate that both the giver and the receiver are no more....)

Earlier, she'd favoured the perfume of Intimate or Chanel No 5! She was loyal to her brands. Her toothpaste was always Colgate, her bathing soap, always Mysore Sandal! She loved the little, simple things oh, so much! For all those who knew Ma, the Lopchu tea leaves would forever be associated with her. She even carried her tea-bags to guests' places, rather than take the tea that they had prepared. As I wrote earlier, tact was not one of her strengths!

Ma was a home- maker in the truest sense of the word. The bricks and cement structure of the house, wherever she lived, turned magically into a home under her TLC! Tantalizing aroma wafted from the kitchen, the furniture sparkled free of all dust, our clothes were always freshly laundered and she was always there to welcome us on our return from school. Ma was like a warm comforter, who blew away the cobwebs of doubt and fear and insecurity. This thin, fragile person was our mainstay. Ma was home, home was Ma! I never imagined it without her, I couldn't!

Ma would make our birthdays special for us. How was she able to do so much! The endless variety of lip-smacking goodies–samosas, sandwiches, chhole, chutneys, gulab-jamun, breadrolls, shahi-toast and the gorgeous, icing-covered, splendidly decorated birthday cake! Looking back, I feel like genuflecting before her again and again in awe and gratitude. How she must have slaved from morning to evening to bring the day to its fruition! And this, not once but thrice a year, year after year after year!

Ma's birthday parties were the talk of the colony. I remember the table laden with food, the drawing room, colorfully alive with streamers and balloons, the laughter and chatter of hundreds of voices, the bustle of friends and family, the huge stack of glittering presents! What a gift Ma gave us! The memories of those events give me a warm glow, even today, almost 40 years later. That's how special Ma made them for us.

Words fail me, Ma! I do not, cannot, believe, God made another like you!

I know Ma was not really very healthy. With her meagre intake of meals, it was hardly possible for her to be entirely without certain health issues.

She suffered from severe attacks of migraine; she would lie in the darkness of the room for two or three days before she completely recovered and she always emerged in a weakened state, seeming more fragile than ever. I remember the long hours that I spent soothing her forehead, trying to ease her pain, wishing childishly and fervently for it to go away. The medicines and treatment only brought her temporary relief. That's about the only time that we saw her take to the bed.

Ma was indefatigable. She ate like a bird and lord knows where she found the energy to accomplish so much in a day. From sun up to sundown to late night, she flitted from one room to the other. The kitchen, of course, was her favorite place and cooking her passion, and she would churn out dish after dish during meal times, each more delicious than the one before. If she enjoyed a dish at a guest's, she would ask for the recipe and then, giving it her own unique touch, would make it taste better than the original! That's what happened with her 'dosas' and 'sambar'; she generously gave credit to Menon aunty for showing her the ropes, but with the way Ma prepared South Indian food I'm very certain even Menon aunty would've taken a bow ! Linda's pizzas never tasted as delicious as Ma's though it was the former who had first treated us to them. Learning and perfecting an art was Ma's forte. I don't know who the patron saint of cooking is, but I'm certain, he sat by Ma when she prepared her 'gajar ka halwa', 'makhane ki kheer', 'gujhiya' or her divine 'gulab jamuns'! I've had them at dozens of places but it was only Ma's magic that could turn these dishes into ambrosia! I wish I had a dram of what she possessed. I'd be a far better person for it.

Ma did not reveal any apparent fears of bogeymen or 'things that go bump in the night'! Once, she'd shared with me her clandestine visit, with a friend, to 'Bhainsakund', the cremation ground. This was when she'd been in college and curious to know why women were discouraged, at times even prohibited, from attending funerals here. Lucknow, in those days, had not spread its tentacles in all directions like a giant, unwieldy octopus. The ground had been on the periphery of the city then and quite isolated, but Ma had felt no unease or apprehension as she sat there. 'So, this is where it all ends', was the thought that had come to her. Phantoms and spooks were nebulous, indefinable to her. 'I'm more afraid of thieves, cutthroats and murderers,' she often admitted in her usual unflappable manner.

She did give proof of possessing nerves of steel (if it was ever required!) on our journey back from Nasirabad. We'd gone to visit Bishun Mama who was posted with the MES in the early 90s. None of us had the slightest inkling of the peril that awaited us. The train journey itself began uneventfully, though the emptiness of the coach was a little unnerving. A couple of stops later, as if to heighten the sense of foreboding, a group of young boys came aboard and showing obvious signs of inebriation spread themselves in the vacant spaces. The lewd and objectionable comments came soon enough. One can only gauge Ma's fears with three young girls (Amrita, Gunjan and me) in her charge. With all the dignity she could muster, she calmly approached an elderly lady in the women's compartment, requesting her to let us in. To her credit, the woman did so with alacrity. The men were enraged at the turn of events and were almost feral in the way they rattled the doors of the closed coupe, laughing drunkenly all the while. Ma asked for my dupatta and fastened the handle of the door more firmly to the berth. It was a long night and Ma sat vigil in the darkness, telling us in reassuring tones, 'Don't worry. Kuch nahi hoga'. And amidst the trepidation, the shivering and fervent praying, I knew that we indeed had nothing to worry. Today, as I sit and recollect those dreadful moments of 25 some years ago, I'm convinced, it was the strength of her aura that had prevailed, that the petty horrors of the night could not have withstood the magnificent courage with which she was imbued.

It was quite quite confounding how she enjoyed TV programmes (very sparingly, though) which were decidedly lurid in content with their conspiracies, violent stratagems, unholy liaisons, et al. This sat so at variance with Ma's composed and prosaic demeanour.

Ma's world revolved around Papa, her kids, Dadi, her home.... all her energy was spent to make life fulfilling and complete for them. My world was Ma, there were times when I couldn't think beyond her. Frankly, I couldn't envisage a life without her. She could do no wrong. She was my moral compass. She was my anchor, my strength. I remember a time in Ranchi when I'd been alone at home. Ma had gone to a neighbor's. When I heard the gate clang and saw a man, who I dreaded, enter, I rushed to the phone, desperately urging Ma to come back. Ma, slim and all of 72 pounds, was my ultimate Chinese wall between me and this lecherous, obnoxious man who was at the gate. She came home running and I cried tears of relief.

Once, when I'd been much younger, maybe four or five, I lay sleepless under the mosquito net. It must have been eleven at night, but some nameless fear kept me awake. Even with Pikku and Dadi in the room, I couldn't play down the morbid thoughts that prevented me from dozing off. My throat dry with terror I whispered again and again-'Mummy'; of course, in the adjacent room, Ma couldn't have heard me even if I'd called out at a normal volume. And suddenly, as if by magic, a soothing hand lay on my forehead. Ma had come. How had she known that her little girl had been afraid and wanted to be comforted! To this day, I have no explanation for what happened. Suffice to say that a mother's instinct to know her children's feelings is an inbuilt mechanism that defies all logic.

Moderation was Ma's mantra. She had no excesses whatsoever, and so, was genuinely shocked at others, who could not resist a vice, be it smoking or alcohol, or anything as unhealthy or unpleasant.

She was a frugal eater. What she didn't like would make for a very long list indeed. I never, in her entire life, saw her have lunch. Everyone would have dal, roti, vegetables, rice and she would have a plate of sliced cucumber! That was HER lunch; at dinner, a roti and a little side dish of vegetables was all she was able to eat; a morsel of gajak or a few spoonfuls of 'boondi' was dessert and she was done! We called her a wonder of nature. A grown human being running on the diet of a bird! And so her weight varied between 30 and 35 and her waist-line never went beyond 21!

One painful fact which all of us will have to accept is though we loved Ma, we never took her word seriously. On hindsight, she'd always turned out to be right, but at the time, she was always ignored. She had implored Papa not to leave England and instead to bring Chacha there for his treatment. Papa went against her–all of us did–and made one of the biggest mistakes of his life. Today, he admits it, regrets it and apologizes to her, when she's no longer present to accept it. Life's ironies come back to hurt us all at one time or the other. You never know what you've got until it's gone. Ma had always had the foresight to know how the consequences of an action would or could pan out. Her prescience was never valued and I believe she felt undermined and slighted, at times. I could sometimes see that defeated look in her eyes but, we are too thick-skinned and obstinate to take cognizance of another point of view if it sits at variance with our own. Therein lies our fault.

Tuesdays were special for Ma. Since she'd been a girl, she'd been devoted to lord Hanuman. Despite her diet, she kept a fast on the day and for some years now had given up taking salt altogether on Tuesdays. Pooja time would be extended by an hour as she would read the Sundarkand along with the Hanuman Chalisa. Then, we would all be given 'prasad' of dry fruits. 'Boondi' would be offered in the evening. This ritual rarely varied and we had grown into the tradition of observing Tuesdays too; no one ate eggs and meat was completely forbidden. All of this, if violated, displeased Ma intensely and no one wished to face her wrath, silent and ominous as it was.

Fasts somehow never made Ma feel listless or weak. Whether it was the Navratris or the difficult 'nirjal' 'Karwa Chauth', she seemed more zestful and ebullient than ever, if possible. She applied herself busily to work on the occasions, preparing the special 'Pooja' items throughout the day and claimed to suffer from no hunger pangs or discomfort whatsoever. In earlier years, though, I have seen her struggle through 'Karwa Chauth', due to the infernal migraine attacks but she never gave in to the pain. Only after the moon had risen and she had performed the precious 'Pooja', would she succumb and lie down in exhaustion. I'm sure, Papa realises the love she bore him throughout these years. 'Karwa Chauth' was never a duty for Ma, but always an act of faith and devotion to him for whom she had forsaken her entire family 53 years ago.

For Ma, a little went a long way. She never borrowed, never owed anybody anything and abhorred the idea of being in debt to someone, especially monetarily. She had a knack of running the household on the salary that Papa brought home with an efficiency that is truly admirable. Where she had got such horse sense from is an enigma because such things can't be taught. It had to be intuitive. True, every single penny was gone by the end of the month, but none of it had been wasted. Good nourishing food was always on the table and we were clad in the best cotton fabrics that could be bought. She saved on the tailor's expenditure, because she stitched most of our dresses herself on her Usha machine. I recall the hours that she spent on the sewing and hemming and even the classes that she took to perfect herself. In those earlier years, she always wore blouses she had made herself, with the sleeves reaching to the elbows! Even when the design had gone out of style, her sleeves retained this length and she was mortified if the tailor (later, she had resorted to getting them stitched) made them shorter, even by an inch!

I do not remember wearing cardigans, pullovers or sweaters bought from shops. Before we left for England, all, and I say all, our woollens were knitted by Ma. Throughout the winter months, Ma would be industriously clicking away her needles to produce exceptionally deigned woollens for us–the intricate patterns, the vibrant colors and impeccable knitting – it was perfection manifest! Others in the colony marveled at Ma's dexterity and proficiency. Some of our pullovers were so flawless that many refused to believe that they were not machine – made! Incredibly, the warmth of her hands seemed to have become an indelible part of the wool, so that when I wore it I didn't feel the cold at all.

Even when in financial straits, Ma never made us feel the lack of any essential item at home. There were always eggs, butter, bread and milk for everyone, surf to clean the clothes, all kinds of soaps for the family's use, shoes and slippers and their accessories, and even an occasional outing where we were allowed to buy story books! I don't remember any of our bed sheets or quilts or blankets having patches or being ragged. Everything was spartan but clean and well maintained. It was all Ma. No one could have done it better. She gave us the best life that we could have had as children. Having come from a joint family where she could claim nothing as her own, she had put the stamp of her exceptional individuality in the way that she had made her family and her home. Mild-mannered yet strong-willed, patient, yet determined, she was a person of many paradoxes, not the least being the fount of energy that propelled her almost delicate- boned physique to performing amazing feats of endurance and resilience. Ma, I salute the woman you were!

Ma had never been garrulous; she spoke only when necessary. I remember the silences that we shared as we sat companionably in the covered verandah of our 3 A/3 home at Ranchi. She would be busy with her knitting or some unending kitchen chore while I was invariably with a book, ruining my eyes further! Only occasionally would she look at me and chide me for my incessant reading. There are so many things I learnt from her through these moments. While she was intent with the task at hand, I would surreptitiously be watching the deft way her fingers shelled the peas or chopped the vegetables; she taught me to chop 'gobhi ka saag' in the finest manner possible to extract its flavour to the maximum when cooked.

Her patience and commitment in accomplishing the smallest of tasks was astonishing. No wonder her cooking was such a revelation. She brooked no shortcuts and had no tolerance for a job hastily or shoddily done. I can understand some people who go about doing their work with perhaps similar dedication and attention, but Ma did it for 53 years without cutting corners, ever! That is phenomenal!

It was in 1977 that Papa got a midnight call from Sharma uncle in Detroit. They'd been great friends before uncle had emigrated to the US. Friendship beckoned and Ma and Papa were sent tickets to go visit them for a three month stay. It was my first separation from Ma and being the oldest, I felt it the most. Though Chacha's family had come down to Ranchi to keep us company, it was no compensation for Ma's absence. Whenever, Papa and Ma called from the US, I could hardly speak for the tears choking me up!

Eventually, the three month stay was cut short by half (whatever may have been the real reason), because, we were being missed too much by our parents. I recall our impatience at the platform, waiting for the train that was bringing Papa and Ma home, and the way I had hurled myself at Ma, clinging to her saree as she'd stepped off the compartment. My god, her feel, her touch, her smell..... my paradise had been right there in her arms; she looked smart and pretty in her new haircut, glamorous even. On reaching home, I tried to emulate the style by chopping off my hair and making a mess of it. I was twelve and mortified at the way the strands stuck out like pine-needles. Again, it was Ma who smoothed them down and pacified me by saying that my hair was thick and straight and had a beauty of its own. Only Ma could make me feel better when the mirror said I looked a right idiot! Until I left to join Mody in 2001, that was the second longest that I'd stayed without Ma and it had been a wrench!

Her other interests, outside her family, were of a cerebral nature. She had a profound knowledge of Indian classical music and particularly of her favourite ragas. She loved to listen to Malkauns and Pahari. She had a sweet voice and sang mellifluously, one thing I've inherited from her! She was always sore at the fact that I did not apply myself to the music lessons with adequate diligence or willingness.

With a fairly pragmatic temperament, Ma never claimed to have been bowled over by anyone from the celluloid world as many of her age had, but she confessed to have been an avid admirer of Sitar maestro, Ravi Shankar. During one bout of spring cleaning, we'd come across a picture of a young Ravi Shankar that she'd kept in a folder. I'd teased her mercilessly about it until she'd turned around and squarely told me it was nothing like my manic obsession for Steve Waugh. That had shut me up!

She loved listening to Pt. Bhimsen Joshi and Pt. D.V. Paluskar. Papa and she would occasionally attend all night SPIC MACAY concerts in BIT, Mesra, coming home in the early hours of the morning. Her taste, even in movies, ran to songs which were based purely on 'ragas'. In her tiny, little diary, she has the lyrics of soulful Lata Mangeshkar numbers from 'Anpadh' and 'Anarkali', or Surraiya and someone called Shanta Apte. Her most favoured male singer was Talat Mahmood and somehow, that doesn't surprise me at all. For the quiet, soft-spoken, sensitive person that she'd been, Talat was the obvious choice! I'd made a collection of her favourite Talat songs last summer and she sat and listened to them with pleasure, humming in an undertone, reliving perhaps, some forgotten moments of her past. There had been a lost, dreamy look in her eyes, and I'd felt, it would have been an intrusion to ask her the reason for it.

She had completed fifth year Sitar Visharad from Bhatkhande but, unfortunately, I never heard her play the Sitar, though, the instrument kept standing for many years in the corner of our store room. Once I'd asked her about it and she had a sad look in her eyes when she said, 'Your Papa doesn't seem very keen.' I was young and felt a spurt of anger against Papa who had robbed Ma of the joy of playing the Sitar. Ma's feelings on the matter were never properly expressed. On certain issues, I feel, she'd been extremely reticent, especially if it would have projected Papa in a poor light. He'd been her knight in shining armor who'd whisked her away from a life of loneliness and neglect and she would do only that which made him happy. Her metier was to be a mother and wife par excellence, a role that she fulfilled effortlessly. Dadi had once also vouched for the fact that she was a daughter-in-law who everyone dreams of and never finds. Dadi and Ma had been a perfect complement to each other. She was the daughter Dadi never had and Ma never missed her own mother, having found a perfect one in Dadi.

I find that there is no particular sequence to this narrative and, even I later, could find myself getting disoriented going through it all. In my defense all I can say is that I had no time to clinically plot it all out into some semblance of orderliness, so that there could have been a harmonious pattern to the events as they unfolded. My mind is a jumble of memories and there is too much pain and trauma for me to have detailed any of this out. So here it all is, in all its fragmented messiness. I hope, Ma forgives me for it, because she, after all, had been the very epitome of meticulousness and propriety.

I know, I cannot avert the inevitable. At some point during this account, I would be forced to dwell on the last days of Ma among us. I also realize that if I avoid doing so, the catharsis that I so desperately yearn for may never come.

I had looked forward to going back home for the ten-day Diwali break. Home was Ma, always and unconditionally, Ma. As she'd done for 15 long years, she stood in the drive-way opening up her arms as I stepped through the gates into them. I hugged her tenderly, gingerly even, and said what I felt, "You've become even thinner, if that's possible!" She brushed the concern aside and I more fool I, did the same. A couple of days before Diwali, she began to complain of pain in the chest. Everyone assumed, including her, that she must've slept the wrong way or pulled a muscle. Some painkillers, a hot water bag and an ointment brought some relief and she was on the go, once again. However, the pain stayed and at times, became too intense for us to ignore it. An X -Ray and ECG were done and to our relief, neither showed any abnormality. We visited a reputed orthopedic physician and, on viewing the X -Ray film, he told us that Ma suffered from a most severe deficiency of calcium and that there were tiny, multiple breakages in her ribcage and shoulders. Seeing the look of alarm in my face, he reassured us that he would try to control the damage but Ma would need to take a lot of calcium in her meals, besides the meds that he was prescribing. We returned home in a buoyant mood, already feeling better. On the way, she even asked me to buy a kilo of apples, the hard kind, and kept reciting all the things she could have which had calcium in them.

On the 5th of Nov., though still in some discomfort, she sat with Deepa mausi's family, chatting, having dinner, posing for photos........ As I look at them now, at her smile that, almost certainly must have hid her pain, I whisper, 'My brave Ma!' Two days later, she bemoaned not being able to prepare 'suji ka halwa' on Adi's birthday. With Gunjan also suffering from typhoid, the holidays had not been festive at all. I was to depart on the 7th from the venue of Adi's party though I did not much relish the thought of leaving, what with both Ma and Gunjan unwell. However, certain pressing work back at Mody forced me to return; I did drop a mail to my Head that, if required, I would have to come back home after the function at School was over. Feeling the hot unshed tears burn my eyes, I hugged Ma goodbye and when she whispered, 'Kab aaogi" I held her tighter and answered, "Jaab bhi tum bulaogi". For the next three days, through the whirlwind of events at the work place, I could only call home briefly to inquire of the patients' condition. There was no cause for worry. Recovery was slow but taking place. The band of tension around my forehead began to relax.

Sunday morning, on the 13th, I woke to the strident notes of Gunjan's phone call. 'Come home, di, Ma is in ICU.' The blood drained from my face and I felt I would fall if I got off the bed. How could this have happened, when I'd been receiving such encouraging reports on her health! Through bits and pieces, I learnt that she had taken a bath that she shouldn't have, which had aggravated her chest pains to the extent that she couldn't breathe properly. Every desperate gasp for oxygen sent slivers of shooting pain through her ribs. A second X-ray revealed the thick spread of pnuemonia over her lungs.

All through the bus journey, on the advice of well-wishers, I chanted the magic mantra of 'Om Namah Shivay' over and over again, hoping, praying, desperately wishing for Ma's speedy recovery. Gunjan and I clasped each other tightly, each trying to instill courage into the other. The drive-way looked forlorn in the absence of Ma. She was far away in a hospital bed, fighting for her life. After a quick bath and change of clothes, we called a cab and reached the medical center where she was in a closed cubicle on the first floor.

I was shocked at her appearance, though I desperately attempted to wear a normal expression and tone as I clasped her hand. Her eyes seemed listless as she breathed tortuously through the oxygen mask. The monitor beeped in the corner, displaying her vital signs. Blood pressure normal, pulse normal, oxygen saturation good (with the mask on, with it off, it started to decelerate). She spoke weakly but ate a few spoonfuls of porridge from my hands and later, even some tea and biscuits. A team of doctors came and pronounced that Ma was responding to the treatment. Recovery would take time because of the general weakness that had never given her a very robust constitution at any point of her life.

Papa, Gunjan, Mama, Mami had all come visiting and even as everyone spoke in murmurs, Ma fell into a fitful sleep and at seven in the evening, most of the visitors left, preparing to come the following day. Mami kept me company. I had no intention of leaving Ma's side. I stood looking down at her, willing her to become better. She had promised me that she would allow me to feed her some 'lauki' and half a chapati later; Pikku left to get this meagre dinner prepared for her and I sat on the cot, soothing her swollen forearm, taped with a syringe plunged through her skin. Her fingers, hands and toes had swollen to such an extent that they were unrecognizable as Ma's. Where were the thin, bony digits through which the veins had always been clearly visible? At times, the skin would be stretched so tightly over them that we could even see the blood coursing through them. These puffy hands and feet seemed to belong to a stranger. No wonder, a little earlier, she had asked me to wear her gold bangles–they were cutting into her distended wrists. Ma and I had always shared the two pairs. She wore it with glass bangles and I without. Now, all four were on my wrist. But not for long, I told myself silently;

only as long as Ma was in the hospital. Once she was back home, the bangles would go right where they belonged.

Abhijeet kept reminding us that Ma should be in respiratory care unit because, her condition was basically lung related. She was, after all, in the gastro-enterology ward that catered to specific problems of the stomach and liver. There was talk of shifting Ma to SGPGI for further treatment the following day. I don't know what happened in the next half hour. Her placid breathing suddenly turned erratic. She moaned, once, twice and panic – stricken, I gasped, crying, "Kya hua, Ma?" Through the labored breathing, she slowly turned her eyes to mine, and even as I began desperately to scream, I saw the light go out of them, I saw them become still...... the next hour was a nightmare. Doctors, paramedics, attendants rushed to administer CPR to her lifeless body, forcing her heart to beat again, her pulse to throb again. My knees gave way, my teeth chattered and my mind became blank. This couldn't be, couldn't be... what about the mantra of Om Namah Shivay" that was supposed to have made her whole again!! Where were the Gods? Why didn't the prayers work? What else could we have done? There were no answers. I had not expected any.

As Ma was shifted into the ICU again, (a futile exercise, I feel, on looking back), Papa and Pikku rushed inside, wonderment and disbelief writ large on their faces. Ma was in a hurry to leave. Nothing worked. All night, Mami, Pikku and I stayed in Abhijeet's chamber but, I knew, even praying now would be of no use. Accepting the reality was not an option either. I remained in the twilight zone of semi consciousness and acuity, not believing what was happening, yet sobbing uncontrollably. This was Ma, my mother, who had been my strength and support for as long as I can remember. How could she just leave in this way? People get a chance to say their good-byes, to settle their accounts, to prepare their loved ones for the final moments.... they don't say they'll have 'lauki and roti' and slip away into oblivion, never to return!

When she was being shifted to PGI on the 15th, the terrifying siren of the ambulance cutting a swathe through the thick traffic, some foolish noise in my head continued to hope. Even the doctors had said the magic words 'miracles happen.'

But this time, the miracle didn't happen. I will never forget, as long as I live, the stark corridor where I sat with Mami and Mintoo, the words that were yelled from one end of it, 'Bed No 8, Malti Bhatt!' With trembling legs, supported by Mintoo, I went up the stairs and entered the Critical Care Unit where Ma lay, tubes and bandages and tapes all over her crushed, defeated, wasted form. I heard the fatal words- 'It is over,' coming from somewhere near my head and I fell at Ma's feet, no longer able to stop the wail that rose from my lips, a lament that has been made by countless men and women as they have lost the dearest, the most loving part of themselves to the inevitable.

My simple, noble, sweet mother was no more....... I'd never understood the finality of death but, in that moment, I knew how bitter its taste can be. It is terrible to find yourself breathing and walking when the most precious part of your life has gone. Many times before, I'd often put this question to myself–what will I do when Ma goes, and I would blithely say nothing, because I won't be alive to suffer the pain. I'll go too; well, that hasn't happened and I'm amazed, even guilt-ridden, at the resilience of life, the tenacity with which it clings to you. It makes you suffer, it makes you want to die, but it doesn't let go of its hold on you.

My eyes felt as though they would burst through the sockets and my lungs gulped in oxygen, even as Ma lay in the sterile, unfeeling medical unit upstairs. I just wanted to take her home, sit by her side, and bathe her lifeless body with my tears.

Pikku brought her back and lay her on a bed of ice. Her face was serene. The vestiges of pain were no more. The following morning, she began her final journey. We dressed her in a resplendent red saree and maroon chunri, decorating her from head to toe, even as the tears streamed unchecked down our faces. This wasn't to be! This isn't why I'd come home – it'd been here to take care of her, nurse her back to health.

The rituals followed–the Puja, the havan, the crowd of friends and relatives, the condolences, the wisdom and the platitudes–nothing brought relief. There was no closure. Life, in all its harshness, opened up like a long, unending path before me, an invisible hand pushing me on to it–go, walk........ and all I wanted to do was sit in a corner and slowly become a part of the wall behind me.

Then, the faces slowly fell into focus; Papa, alone and suddenly shrunk in stature, appearing lost and vulnerable. His partner had left him just short of their 54th marriage anniversary. The Royal Bengal Tiger had aged visibly in 48 hours and the fearsomeness that had been so much a part of his persona, seemed like a mirage. Looking at him, I understood the nature of my own selfish grieving. Papa's loss was the greatest, especially when I recalled the way he had won Ma's affection and fought against the tide of her family's disapproval to make her his own. Their romance of yester years had stood the test of time, had seen tumultuous ups and downs, had overcome the many barriers that would inevitably have come their way and had finally found the calm, unhurried pace of walking together in the twilight of their lives. Now, Papa stood alone on this road, not believing his fate, his eyes restlessly searching for her and his voice echoing just the one word—'Malti, Malti, Malti......... I had to stop my own tears to wipe away his. I must not store my memories in my eyes, they may roll down with tears. I must store them in my heart, so that every heartbeat reminds me of their beauty.

My memories flow on... Ma's boundless source of energy had been a conundrum none of us have been able to solve. Her daily diet included three large mugs of tea, devoid of all milk and sugar and brewed of the finest Lopchu tea- leaves of Darjeeling, a slice of bread over which she generously spread homemade butter and then sprinkled it with the spicy 'dalmot' of Aminabad–this was breakfast! Sliced cucumber or a bowl of curd was lunch. A few 'namkeen' tidbits made up evening tea and a smallish sized 'roti' or 'paratha' with the vegetable of the day was dinner! With a few variations, here or there, this had been her intake for close to 50 years! In retrospect, the only explanation that comes to mind is divine energy. She was propelled by some kind of spiritual strength that never made her lie down to rest during the day, never tired her out, never made her feel weak, never enervated her...... What else could it have been? She was a machine whose engine ran on hardly any fuel at all! I recall those summer afternoons when I returned exhausted from work. After lunch, I would flop down for a siesta while she sat near my pillow and read a book. After a couple of hours of healthy snoozing, when I came awake I'd find her in the same position, reading! I would shake my head in wonder and ask her how she could be so still, keep sitting in that position for so long; and she would smile and tell me all the things she had completed while I'd been resting. The table had been cleared, the dishes emptied, the kitchen cleaned......

My friends and colleagues refused to believe me when I described Ma to them. 'She doesn't seem real' would be their response. Only when they had met her in person were they able to accept the truth of my words. But that didn't mean, they weren't astounded by what they'd seen with their own eyes.

Many came to offer solace at the workplace. Their words and gestures of consolation and sympathy could bring only a tiny modicum of comfort to my heart. How could it be otherwise when it has been torn asunder so? Some asked me how old Ma had been and when I said '80', I could see the incredulity in their expression that plainly said, 'So why this disbelief at her demise, why the unacceptance of the ordained. She was OLD'. But, that's the thing; she was old only chronologically. Her movements, as if in defiance of her age were always very definitive, her manner always upbeat. She brimmed with enterprise, ever in motion, ever sprightly. Even the orthopedic doctor who we'd gone to for a checkup, had exclaimed, '80'! Mataji, you don't look a day over 60! Give me also the herbs that have kept you so young,' bringing a smile to Ma's lips.

How could I explain this singular fact of Ma's personality to those who had never had the good fortune of meeting and knowing her– the exceptional human being that she'd been!

Ma was a stickler for perfection. Either she would not take up a commitment at all, or if she did, she would invariably see it to its completion, come what may. 'Impossible" was not something she believed in; 'Hoga kaise nahi' was her response, always. This is one thing, I hope, I have learned from her. Ma's tuition was very subtle. There were no in your face directions or instructions to accomplish a task; she would do it herself, without asking us to observe her methods, but the intentness and absorption with which she worked were encouragement enough for the learners. I remember her deftness with the knitting needles and having watched her for a while, one day, I begged her to teach me this skill. Under her expert tutelage, I completed two wonderful pullovers for myself.

My handiwork was much appreciated, though I know I had not been able to bring the kind of exquisite neatness that was the hallmark of her knit work! Well, perfection is not easily found. Everywhere, it is at a premium and I had the most beautiful example of it in my Ma!

Ma loved the simple things in life. Not for her intricately carved, gold 'kadas' instead, she kept a dazzling array of glass bangles. She loved them with a passion untold! During my trips to Firozabad, my only personal work would be to browse the market for glass bangles for Ma–red, pink, magenta, orange, maroon–she loved their texture against her wrists and the way they jangled against one another. They would always be a couple of safety pins fastened on to one of them. How many hundreds of time have I borrowed them from her, knowing with certainty, that I would find one there! These little moments have gone forever. There would be no sweet clinking of those glass bangles ever now........

Her second toe would never be without a 'bichia'. She had an assortment of them which she changed from time to time. I remember, how the ends were cutting into her skin as she had lain in the hospital bed because of the swelling in her feet, and even then she forbade me from taking them off. 'Thoda dheela kar do' was what she wanted me to do! This Diwali, she showed me her purchases with pleasure–a beautiful pair of gold bangles, lovely 'bichia' and 'payal'. All of them so, lovingly bought, lie unused, unworn in their boxes. Ma went without being able to wear them. I doubt, any of us will ever muster the courage to do so. The flood of memories will be too difficult to check!

Ma hardly had any jewellery to speak of; a few trinkets and some pearls were all I could find in the closet; I'm fairly sure, there is no other secret chamber where she hoarded her treasures. Ma's heart was pure, 24 carat, gold; it was generous, forgiving, honest, simple and huge! When I think of her today, I find strength in the knowledge that I am the daughter of a woman who was as pure as the driven show.......

Some 25 years earlier, Ma had been extremely worried about my marriage. Putul's marriage had already entered the third year and this put her in panic mode. She went about amassing my trousseau. Beautiful sarees (she had impeccable taste!), a couple of gold jewellery sets (again, intricately designed) and a pair of exquisite gold 'kadas' (which I've lost, btw!), cotton bedsheets, designer bed-covers and numerous other knick-knacks. She arranged them all in a suitcase and put my initials on it. Everything was ready except a groom! More than myself, I felt for Ma, and the longing that tore her apart when Rajul, Babli, Amrita and Jaya, all got hitched one after the other. Some things are just not meant to be and I know, there were scars on my mother's soul when things didn't go as planned. If I'm truly honest with myself, I'd say that the experience didn't really hurt me much because Ma stood as a talisman between me and all that was vile and demonic. In her own inimitable way she became my savior. We'd shared the same room in those days and I remember talking late into the night, pouring out the extent of my horrors until I was spent. In her presence, I was cleansed and reborn as a stronger, more confident individual.

It was Ma who urged me to broaden my horizons and start applying outside Lucknow. Without her staunch faith in my ability, I would never have gathered the courage to leave home.

All my life, I suddenly discover my actions have been subconsciously motivated by Ma. Once, some 16 years ago, I had returned late from work. It was December and the days had turned chilly. Looking for Ma, I came to the verandah at the rear of the house and found her struggling to wash out a couple of bed-sheets. Aghast, I asked her what she thought she was doing in the cold water. She looked at me and that was answer enough for me. With my meagre savings, I went the very next day and got a new semi-automatic washing machine, which I'm glad to say, served us very well for close to 12 years. The look of joy on Ma's face is something I cherish to this day. There is another similar incident, when I'd felt I had to prove to Ma how fiercely I loved her. It was near Diwali and we'd just spent the better part of the night without any electricity. When I came out of the room in the morning, I found Ma on all fours, mopping up the large puddle of water in the dining room; the ice had melted from the fridge and overflowed the plate at the bottom. It was painful to watch Ma, because again she was cleaning up the mess so that none of us slipped and hurt ourselves. I went to the same store and ordered the purchase of a frost-free refrigerator to be delivered at the earliest. As luck would have it, it came on the day of Diwali! What a moment that was! Small pleasures of life but the intent behind them was infinitely profound and I believe I saw Ma look at me and nod slightly.

She understood that this was nothing but a small way of showing how much she meant to me. Her joy was my joy. All this was naught compared to what she had given us our entire lives. She had turned us out as decent human beings, who would always be honest to themselves and to their work. She made us understand the importance of the 'here' and 'now'. 'Kal kabhi nahi aata' are words I've heard her say a thousand times and she probably would've said them a hundred more times had she been here, lest we forget their import!

I regret, I could not buy her any new books to read in the past few months. She loved the classics—Premchand, Sarat Chandra, Bankim Chandra, Ashapurna Devi, Bhagwati Charan Verma, Shivaji Sawant, Shivani—her little library had a rich array of titles and she'd yearned to add more to her collection. I kept putting it off, promising to shop for her online. What wouldn't I give today to be able to see her reading a thick book I'd bought her on Amazon, with her spectacles resting on her nose.........my life itself, if that were possible.....

When I look at the photos of Ma of earlier years, I can see why she had caught Papa's fancy. There is a soft vulnerability about her that she more than adequately hides beneath a veneer of tranquility. Her face just falls short of being heart-shaped. Instead, there's greater charm as the chin bears slightly squarish lines. This should have marred the symmetry of her features, but somehow, only gave it a haunting look that stayed with one long after the album was closed shut!

Today, I only have to close my eyes and the sights and sounds of my present melt away and images of Ma fill my senses like never before—her thinning hair is perfectly coiffed, the greys of which had remained deftly coloured right up to her eightieth year! She is just a little stooped with age, having lost none of her verve, though and a one rupee coin sized red 'bindi' sits on the wide expanse of her forehead; a nose-pin winks on the left side of her face and an infinitesimal gap that had appeared between her front teeth is visible as she smiles her brilliant smile in a moment of joy; the ever-present maroon bangles clink softly against her bony wrists; her eyes, alive and brimming with love for me, look into mine, and that fraction of time becomes an eternity as I keep them shut for as long as I can.....

Despite the fragility of her slightly-built physique, there was no hint of emaciation in her face. Ma photographed very well. It seems even the lens of the camera could not help but capture the vitality that was such an integral part of her persona! Her eyes, touched with a hint of grayish-blue, like Mama's, shone with the idea of all that she had to do throughout the day! Sometimes, I'm sure she felt there were not enough hours on the clock for all that she wished to accomplish. It was difficult for us to keep up with the frenetic pace of her work, especially around Diwali, when she would take upon herself to clean and sanitize each and every corner of the house. For days, she would be a-bustle, maniacally pursuing her mission until she was certain she had rid the rooms of all cobwebs, filth, dirt and clutter.

We remember with fondness her manner of reading the morning paper. With her glasses perched precariously on her bridge, she would spread the pages of The Nav Bharat Times over the dining table and, and sipping leisurely on her Lopchu tea, proceed to read the length and breadth of the news of the day. Some days, she would take an hour and a half to peruse the broadsheets, savouring the stories and offering her own analyses on matters political, social, economic or cultural—remarks, I believe, made more to herself than to any of us!

Lately, she'd become a little hard of hearing, (a genetic failing in several members on Ma's side of the family), though to mention it to her was to earn her ire in no uncertain terms. 'Tum log muh udhar karke bologe to kaise sunai dega?' So, actually, it turned out, WE were at fault, she couldn't hear properly! Another job that was set for everyone, at some point of time during the day, would be to look for her glasses! 'Fridge pe hoga. Nahi hai? To telephone ke paas dekh lo. Wahan bhi nahi? Pooja ghar me dekhna...'

Ma, your glasses lie forlorn in their case today; to glance at it is to be reminded of the eyes that had looked through them at the transmutation of life and the relationships they had formed and nurtured over the years.

Ma had been a giver. Always, an irrevocable giver! Even when she'd loathed something, something we may have liked, she would make sure we never went without it. She abhorred the smell of ripe bananas, guavas, mangoes or papaya and always complained of the fridge reeking of them if we kept the fruits in it. But she never dissuaded us from having them; indeed, she even bought them herself for us on many occasions!

I remember her telling me to have a banana on Monday, when I kept a fast. 'Bahut filling hota hai', she'd say and I asked her how she could know that, having never tasted the fruit even once in her life!

She could not take tomatoes in her food, didn't like the taste of them, she said. Yet, she prepared dishes for the family, such as 'aloo-tamatar' or 'baigan ka bharta', where she put in the vegetable in abundance, eating none of it herself and instead, taking immense pleasure in our enjoyment of the dishes.

We have picked up so many of Ma's habits that, at times, it feels a trifle uncanny to watch each other do the exact same things in the exact same way. Ma has managed to ingrain certain practices in us that would be difficult to eschew. Though, to begin with, her efforts had been met with reluctance, criticism, complaint and, at times, open defiance, it did not deter her from doing things the way she considered to be the best. Being quite the dictator in the realm of her kitchen, it was either HER way or no way! Even when a dinner party wound up close to midnight, the crockery had to be washed, dried and put away safely before we could call it a day. 'The masala stains will ruin the china," she reasoned. When tired and frazzled, we wanted to leave them overnight for the maid to clean them the next morning, she would rush to the sink and indicate she'd do the chore herself and we could go to bed if we were so exhausted. (As if, after that, we could've!!). Unwillingly, we would complete the work to her satisfaction, even as the hands of the clock sometimes struck one! Of course, to Ma's credit, she NEVER, ever made us do this alone. It was well nigh unthinkable for her to retire to her room and leave us to struggle with the dirty dishes. She would be beside us, right up to the point where the last plate and bowl were neatly arranged back in the cabinet.

She has drilled into us that the kitchen should be left spotless every night after dinner is over. The gas cooker is scoured with soap water, the tiles and counter swabbed, first with a wet mop and then dried off. The stainless steel sink has no unwashed spoon or glass in it (oh, the horror if it does!) and it is similarly scrubbed with scotchbrite and wiped of all moisture so that it gleams like new when the kitchen light is snapped off! If we ever, henceforth, leave the kitchen in a mess at night, it will seem like sacrilege and I doubt, we will be able to get any sleep at all!

Ma taught us how to take out 'purees', 'samosas' or 'pakoras' from the oil in the pan, once they were done. We could not just drag them to the sides and slice them out on to a plate. 'The oil will ooze down the edges and stick to the underside. It'll take ages to scrub it off," she'd explain. So, she'd make sure the oil was properly strained before the item was lifted out of the pan and transferred to a plate with nary a drop of oil oozing or spilling anywhere. She wouldn't allow Uma Mami or anyone else to help her out with these jobs. 'Nahi, tum kadhai gandi kar dogi,' would be her blunt reply to such overtures. We also had to bear the brunt of her irritation if we made the Vim bar, kept for the washing up, soggy.

She has made all of us understand the benefit of having lukewarm or hot water in the morning, at night, and every time in between. From Punam, to Aru, to me, all have begun to appreciate how right she had been as we follow her example now, especially in the winter months. The first thing every morning and the last at night, we always saw her nursing a glass of piping hot water, up to the very end.

Each one of us goes the extra mile to do things in a way that would have met Ma's approval. It's as if she's watching over us from some vantage point and we're attempting to score brownie points with her by doing so! Oh, I so fervently wish that this were true and she is....

Ma was one of a kind. Everyone who had came to pay their respects, confessed to have been touched by her in some small, indefinable way. Cousins flew in from various parts of the country, even if it was for a day. Ma was no public figure, but all who knew her came to share our grief, even those whom we hadn't met for years. Ma brought us all together again. As in life, so in death!

She loved family gatherings and both 'Rakshabandhan' and 'Bhaiya Dooj' were huge affairs where old and young would converge to spend precious moments together. 'Bhaiya Dooj' would be a much bigger deal than Diwali. Whenever, we suggested that these 'dos' be toned down a trifle, she would bristle and say 'Jab hum nahi honge tab jaise chaho waise karna'! Oh Ma, why did you have say those words!

On her birthday this year, I'd gifted her a Titan wrist watch, studded with American diamonds. Her childlike excitement had been so palpable that it had brought tears to my eyes. There was so much innocence in her. She was so transparent about her joys and sorrows that you couldn't help but be touched by them. I'd teased her with the words 'tum jiyo hazaron saal', and was rather taken aback at her show of displeasure at them. 'Aisi wish mat do, yeh wish karo ki hum chalte firte chale jayen. Kisi ki sewa nahi leni pade.'

And that's the way she went. Here today, gone tomorrow! Like a butterfly or a sparrow, she flitted away to a world unknown taking nothing from us, except our peace of mind, except our happiness! I've heard that only the purest and noblest of souls are blessed with a death that took Ma away from us– so quickly and painlessly. I'm only grateful for the fact that such a gracious and unblemished life was an inextricable part of our own lives.

I feel helpless and torn; I am too far away from my family at this most tragic and wretched moment of our lives. Waves of sorrow engulf me, even as I force myself to take up a piece of work and apply all my faculties to getting it done. It is an uphill and strenuous task, when the mind falters and runs amok, finding comfort in her memories alone.

It is reflexive, not something I can control. She's my last thought as I turn out the lights and wait for the blessed oblivion to descend and the first when the cock shrilly crows me awake at six. I have been desperately praying for her to come into my dreams since 16th Nov. and finally, on the 18th of Dec. she did. I saw her vividly in the puja ghar, standing with her back to me and on hearing me call out to her, turning around. I half expected her to change into someone else…but, it was Ma's lovely face that looked at me. I said 'Ma' in amazement and she walked out of the room. I held on to her tightly. She smiled but said nothing…..I cannot interpret what I saw. I still recall the thrill on waking up and going around for a few hours with the feel of her in my arms.

I know, with time, her memories will become a solid ball of light and lodge itself into the deepest corner of my heart. It will warm me when I'm cold and lonely, show me the way as I travel on this journey of life (that I must). But, at present, this is yet to happen. Very often, now and then, an excruciating sliver of pain and disbelief shoots through me, forcing me to acknowledge the horror of a life without her. I have imaginary conversations with her, urgently holding on to the belief, nay, the faith that she's watching over us, as protectively as she had always done.

Grief is a very private state. I know people mean well when they offer me consolation, but how can anyone know the profundity of another's sorrow! We have different mechanisms, each one of us, to cope with a loss of this magnitude. Some may find relief in the comforting words of others, but for many they remain just words..... 'life has to go on', they say. I know. 'Stay strong'. I know that too. Isn't it a show of strength that I manage to drag myself through the day, accomplishing the work that I have to do, without dissolving into a flood of tears.....? But, when I'm also urged to smile and laugh and be cheerful.....I'm afraid, the very idea nauseates me. Life doesn't hold a great deal of charm for me these days. It is by being strong, as has been demanded of me by so many, that I am able to go on with any measure of equanimity. I'm incapable of anything more than this at this juncture. but I yearn for the day when I too can 'become comfortably numb'......

Gunjan confesses to undergoing similar pain. She refuses to believe the agony will subside with time. She says it will go only when she breathes her last. I agree with her and attempt to give courage to both of us through pitifully inadequate words. It is also true, though, that we do Ma a grave injustice by crying incessantly. She would be appalled to learn how weakly and spinelessly her daughters behaved when the moment of truth came. During crunch time, she would have wanted to us to step into the breach and prove our mettle, not just to the world, but, more importantly to ourselves…………

I think the fact that I remained single made both Gunjan and me cling to Ma like a port in storm. I remained tethered to her even as I grew older, never really imagining that the post might not be there forever. Each time, I faced a setback or confronted an adversity, Ma's reassuring presence was all I'd needed to go beyond and over it. I was taller, heavier, wider than her, but her frailty was only visible in her physical frame. She had a power that we could sense very distinctly in our times of need. She was our bulwark 'against the slings and arrows of outrageous fortune'. Perhaps, it was because I had never seen her lose control over anything at anytime. There had always been a calm, unflinching aura around her that drew an invisible circle of protection for her children, who she loved, unconditionally and completely. She cushioned our fall, patted dry our tears, and pushed us gently yet with an inexorable firmness, to find our feet again, to stand erect. We didn't even know it and later found that a little of her brand of fortitude had been transferred to us, sub rosa….. That was Ma!

I too have inherited the migraine from Ma. Having suffered the splitting headache for close to 40 years, Ma knew what I went through during the attacks. She must've read of some remedy for them, some panacea to cure me of them forever during her protracted devouring of the morning newspaper. On one of my visits home, she'd come with a handkerchief knotted at one end. 'There're some ground cloves here. When the pains come, breathe in the aroma, deeply. It will help.' I keep her 'nuskha in my handbag. If it works it will be because of the care and concern with which it had been prepared. She never stopped being a mother... it was as if I was still ten years old for her and it made it difficult for me to grow up in any real sense. As long as Ma was there, I'd known with certainty there was a buffer if I ever stumbled. Now, I have to take baby steps again. I have to learn to walk again...

Ma was a gift to us from paradise and I believe, we have become better people because we are her flesh and blood. Her meeting with her Maker is just one instant in a full and lovely life and we, as her children, should celebrate rather than mourn her passing. Human nature, being what it is, is rarely able to accept the loss of a loved one with equanimity. All the teachings, wisdom and philosophies of the Gita fall by the wayside, failing to assuage the grief that spills over; I'm waiting though, for the time when I realize that the joy of having basked in the radiance of her presence is far, far greater and ennobling than the sorrow at her quietus....

I wear her sarees everyday to work. In some of them, the creases of when Ma had last worn them still remain and it gives me a wonderfully comforting feeling to drape the fabric around myself. The fragrance that was so uniquely her own clings to me, too and I feel deliriously close to Ma all through the day; so much so that, at times, I cannot see myself as a separate entity at all, but as essentially a part of her...

Today, I think of the most ordinary of things, mundane even, but also see the enchantment that makes them images of beauty–the rising of the sun, the first star in the sky, the rainbow, a butterfly, a rose bud, the smile of an infant, the song of the cuckoo or the sweet fragrance of the 'bela', I think of Ma, for she is all of this for me and more.....With time, they say, the pain would abate, the scars would heal and I will become whole again, but I know, the umbilical cord was never properly cut off. Wherever her soul has gone, the ties still bind me to her and doubtless, they always will.

Rest in peace, Ma, and may peace come soon to me too—-

LOVE.........FOR YOU

When the dawn breaks over the saffron skies,

When the dreams of night slowly leave my eyes,

When the first wild rose blooms among the rushes,

When the air resounds with the songs of thrushes,

When the dark clouds descend in a flood of tears,

When the sounds of silence are all that one hears

When life and love and you seem a part of my past,

When out into the world, like a waif, I am cast,

When the strong gusts of wind make me tremble and sway,

When the power of my thoughts takes me far far away,

When the meaning of truth seems empty and lost,

When the star of my fortunes seems forever to be crossed,

When each new night and day brings tears anew,

I think of you, mother, I only think of you........

(19th March, 1990)

The Oldguard...

January 8, 2017

Long before the advent of the internet and eons before the modern teaching-learning methodology evolved, the best and in my opinion, the only ways were to learn from either experimenting or observing & emulating our elders. People those days may not have been as qualified as today's generation in the use of modern gadgetry or the world may not have been a small entity, the Concept of global village might have been a really far-fetched notion, they may not have been as suave, polished & glib but they knew ENOUGH.

They understood how the world went around, they realized the value of life, virtues of patience, honesty, loyalty, respect, hardwork & perseverance. They experienced what it was to work hard and yet lose when their efforts were pit against divine & natural deterrents. They fathomed how to win against insurmountable odds. They appreciated that their children will model after them & their behavior. They discerned that they were the lighthouses that would steer the navigators of the future to a safe & sure shore. They stood witness to a society brought up on so many virtues of good living. Their resolve, when put against adversities was exemplary. Rarely ever, were they perturbed with the bouncers that life so unerringly threw at them. They were Pure Gold-those people, who inhabited our planet just a generation back.

Many of them, aging & ailing though they may be, are still around. Sadly, we have sidelined their wisdom, forced them behind margins made by us-the freshly educated, tech-savvy, modern generation. Nearly all of us are guilty of undermining their advice and guidance from time to time. "You don't know how the world works these days", is the constant litany of the young & their easy excuse to escape the transgression of disregarding the oldguard- the parents & the grandparents.

Time & again, our Oldguard gives us glimpses of their tough veneer & highly virtuous moral fibre, that they cherish above all and that has stood them in good stead all their lives. And in so doing, help us pull ourselves out of the quagmire of doubt, stress, dishonesty, low self-esteem and an ebbing confidence in the sustainability of our very lives.

This afternoon, I was faced with one such low, having lost a much needed sum of money. I learnt an important lesson today. No matter how listless and uninterested our aging parents may be in the daily nitty-gritty of this fast paced digital life, they still hold the aces when it comes to being calm & composed when faced with life's challenges. Here I was, lamenting the loss of a hefty (for me) twenty five thousand to thieves (girls, if I may add), wondering how were we going to manage our immediate needs and then there were my parents – my father, a septuagenerian & my mother well in her sixties, tranquil & even-tempered. I realised that they must have been perturbed deep down yet remaining unruffled for our sakes was their biggest gift to us. Without making a conscious effort, they bestowed a valuable life lesson to us, merely by example.

My mother told me this evening, "what is gone is gone, may be it never was meant to be yours in the first place. Make all the efforts you need to, in order to retrieve what you have lost but then if you don't recover it, just let it be. Don't waste your days & spoil a good night's sleep, moping, sulking & bewailing the loss of something that cannot be reclaimed. 'What ifs' just bring in misery & wretchedness. Crying over it won't help. It will just cloud your judgement and prevent you from finding a way out."

Such wise words, spoken with such candor, with such Simplicity..

We are life long learners and we would do well to accord that, much-needed deference, honor, esteem, regard & attention bordering on reverence to our Oldguard. They truly, have been and still are the torch-bearers of our time-honored wisdom & sagacity.

For hardships and how to deal with them, Master Rumi puts it aptly-

Don't be Sad! God sends Hope in the most desperate moments. The heaviest rain comes out of the darkest Clouds.

Why Write?

April 22, 2017

I came across these beautiful lines on the internet today and couldn't resist sharing.. If I put my heart into it, I can give a million other reasons Why to Write but I guess these lines pretty much sum it all up..

Write because you want to communicate with yourself.

Write because you want to communicate with someone else.

Write because life is weird and tragic and amazing.

Write because talking is difficult.

Write because it polishes the heart.

Write because there is a blackbird outside of my window right now and oh my god isn't that the best start to the day?

Write because you're trying to figure yourself out.

Write because you might not ever figure yourself out.

Write because there still aren't enough love poems in the world.

Write because everything is not always talked about.

Write because some things are left unspoken.

Write because it calms your soul.

Write because it rests your mind.

Write because you don't have a friend who understands.

Write because you have a lover who understands.

Write because words are necessary to paint the unnecessary things in life.

Write because words don't go wasted.

Write because life is too delicious to not be tasted.

Write because no one can ever understand your messy mind.

Write because there's a lot of poetry and songs in your heart.

Write because your words can strengthen someone's life and yours as well.

Write because you have a lot to say and nobody is there to listen to you.

Write because words can feed your soul..

Write so that All is not Lost…

Crack

May 2, 2017

An ambiguous title, I agree!! But it was infact, A Crack that inspired me to crack open the mystery of my mind and take a crack at unravelling what turbulence lay beneath the presumably calm and quiet disposition that I portray despite being perturbed to the very core.

Last night, I was deranged to the point of being depressed and anxious. There might have been many factors attributing to that state of mind. I know I had read something that left a deep impact, an indelible imprint on my mind, may be it were the events, the people around, the presence or absence of some, the sudden realisation of a loss, a mental check and balance of life's wear and tear.

As long as there is life, there'll be no shortage of reasons. Whatever it was, it threw me off balance. I had a restless night, a cranky morning and because I had to drive around 300kms, a very tiring journey.

I was exhausted by the way my mind kept churning out thoughts after thoughts, some complete others partial & half-formed, with no seemingly set pattern or precedent attached to them. There was a stretch of road on my way where I drove at about a 140kms/hour, all the while thinking, what if I ram this car into an oncoming vehicle and summarily dismissing the insane idea. That's how irrelevant things got.

But, you see, the human mind is a tricky thing. It is as layered as it is complex. It poses questions which might not have simple solutions or may be they do but are hard for us to see & fathom. At times, our mind provides resolutions when least expected. I have increasingly come to relate the inner design of my mind to the intricate interlacing of ribs in a spider's web. I love the term mental cobwebs when used for my confused state of mind. Nevertheless, it would be negative of me to call it a cobweb because while the latter are deserted, dust-laden, abandoned structures, the former serves a tangible purpose of feeding the Creator. Both have an innate beauty. Both, works of art! One has life the other has outlived its life's aim.

Coming back to my muddled thoughts and the sudden stroke of inspiration or light it received. While driving at this outrageous speed, a small pebble flew and hit my car's windshield leaving a miniscule yet discernible CRACK on it. The tracery or the form that emerged right before my eyes had so much visual conformity with the spiral, orb- like way a spider spins its web or to be precise the plight my mind was in, at that particular moment, that instantly all my attention converged onto it. It was like a giant jigsaw, with all its pieces finally falling into place.

Straightaway, I mellowed down. Something had clicked into place like the right key for the lock. I was perceptibly more relaxed, pacified & at peace. I could finally, comprehend & make sense of my disquiet and conceive a way out. The cloud had cleared, rightaway. The spectre of doom that so overshadowed my reason, had lifted. I realised the fallacy of my conduct & thoughts.

I realised that life is for the living and that it will go on whether the people you love or choose to be with, stay or not. It will not stop even if there are errors in your judgement. You will continue to breath, in failure or success, alike.

Crumbling in the face of disagreements, inconveniences, losses or discomforts is easy. What is tough, is holding on, being courageous and letting go!! What is commendable is making something of yourself against all odds, controlling your mind & heart, not the other way round!!

Contemplating is wise & logical. Overthinking and suffering due to that, isn't. 'What ifs' bring nothing but chaos. Whatever happens, happens for the best. I know it is a cliché but there is always something better, hidden in the ways of the universe. Losing hope and sanity is not an option. Last but not the least, ACCEPTANCE is the way to go. Once we accept things as they are, there is a lot less pain, a lot less expectation and a lot more forgiveness.

It was Rumi who said, "A wound is the place the light enters you."

Leonard Cohen developed it into an anthem that goes like this~

The birds, they sang at the break of day
I heard them say – Don't dwell on what has passed away
Or what is yet to be
Ah, the wars they will be fought again
The holy dove, she will be caught again

Bought and sold and bought again
The dove is never free
Ring the bells that still can ring
Forget your perfect offering
There is a crack, a crack in everything
That's how the light gets in

We asked for signs, the signs were sent
The birth betrayed, the marriage spent
Yeah, the widowhood of every government
Signs for all to see
I can't run no more with that lawless crowd
While the killers in high places say their prayers out loud
But they've summoned, they've summoned up a thundercloud
And they're going to hear from me
Ring the bells that still can ring
Forget your perfect offering
There is a crack, a crack in everything
That's how the light gets in
You can add up the parts, you won't have the sum
You can strike up the march, there is no drum
Every heart, every heart to love will come But like a refugee
Ring the bells that still can ring
Forget your perfect offering
There is a crack, a crack in everything
That's how the light gets in

Ring the bells that still can ring
Forget your perfect offering
There is a crack, a crack in everything
That's how the light gets in
That's how the light gets in
That's how the light gets in.

At War...

May 4, 2017

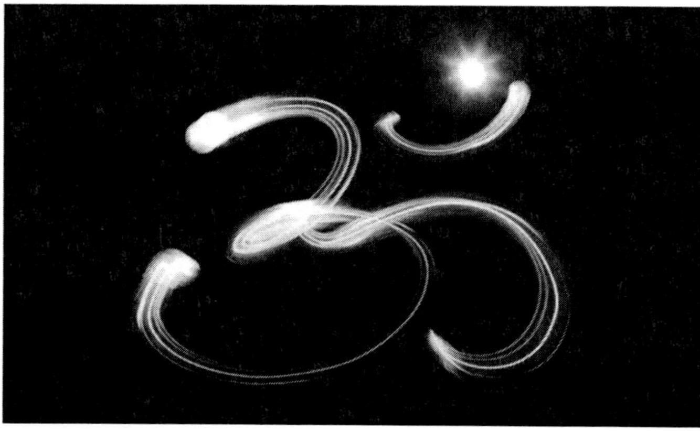

For all those familiar with Margaret Mitchell's Gone with the Wind, the scenario I am about to mention won't be new.

It was in this classic that we came across the grit and solidarity of the Southern women, ladies or otherwise. In a much loved scene, that happens many times over, the ladies of the household & neighborhood would sit together in any one of their homes and talk about mundane stuff, sewing or knitting, all the while actually waiting, eagerly, for any news from the front. They would sit and chat and backbite and criticise yet their minds would be preoccupied with the well-being of their men out to fight the Civil War.

I experienced something like that today when we, my mom & I, visited my uncle's place. The ladies of the family were all present, putting up a brave front, chatting about routine, everyday things, reinstating their faith in the almighty, serving tea and snacks to visitors; all the while waiting, keenly, for news or update from the hospital, where my uncle is battling the inevitable.

It's a war against Death; a war against anything that threatens one's belief in God; a war for faith; a war for love, for family, for children. For the first time in my life, I hope that faith wins, that God persists, that life sustains..

May he win his battle against an inescapable destiny.. May life triumph..

For as long as he is breathing, there is HOPE..

Hoping for a Miracle!!

Need all your prayers..

Choices

May 26, 2017

I went to the general store the other day and decided, on an impulse, to get a different brand of tooth paste for myself. It was weird and at the same time exciting to add it to my cart, after all, for as long as I can remember, I have been using the same brand of toothpaste, the same red color, the same taste. This morning while finally opening the new tube of shiny yellow green paste with cooling crystals, I felt like an adventurer out on her maiden voyage into the unknown..

Great things never came from comfort zones.

Hilarious as it may sound, most of us don't venture out of our habits and comfort zones even for something as mundane as a new kind of toothpaste. It's not brand fixation that keeps us tied up, atleast not in my case. It is just the comfort of the familiar.

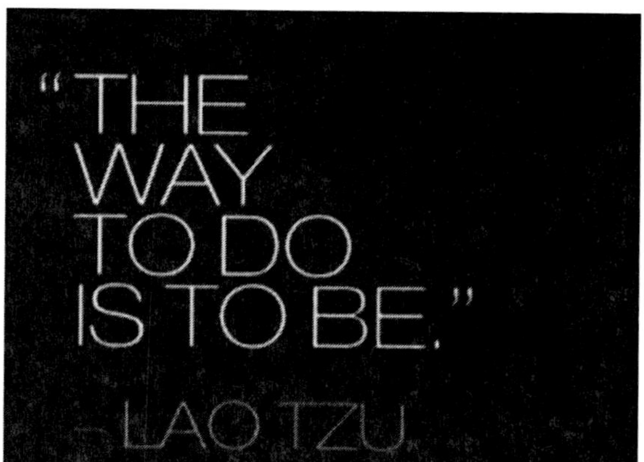

Sadly enough, consumer products are just an example of what we are doing with our lives. I cannot speak for everyone, neither can I generalise (I hate to generalise, as it is). But I have to write about what sparked this seemingly unremarkable or ordinary sounding thought process.

FIND YOURSELF

and be that

I read quotes like – "Life isn't supposed to be lived in one place." – and being a thinking person I understand how right that is, both geographically and intellectually. One has to travel, one has to explore, gain new experiences, let go of the things and people gone by.. One has to grow.. And people don't grow while being confined to their comfort zones.

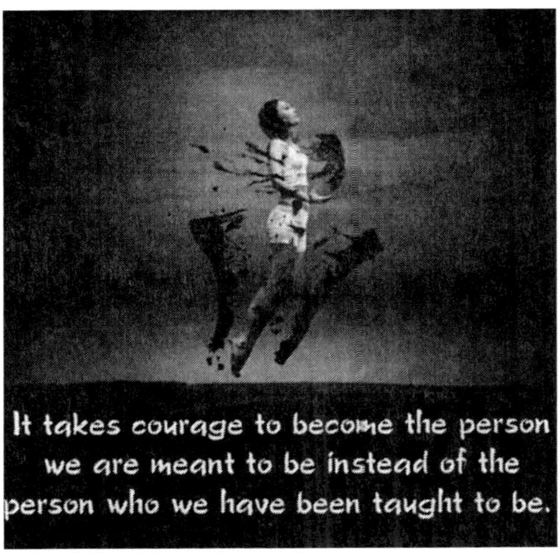

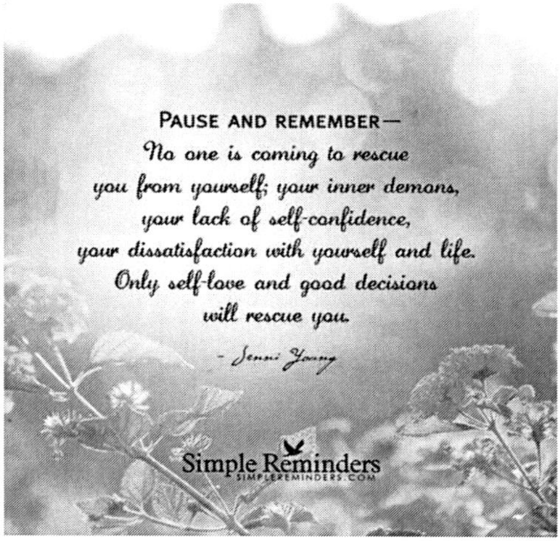

One has to try different things, be different people in order to find what one actually is. Experimenting, juggling choices, failing, learning in the process- Everything is important.

While I know all this theoretically, I have never dared to try my luck outside the protective cocoon of my family. I cannot remember a time when I wasn't told what to do and how to do it. A set of instructions were always provided no matter what I decided to do. I understood quite early in my life that simply following the instructions provided, would save a lot of bad blood and complications. I did not know any other way to live.

I had never learnt to live without my support structure. I had never been to a bank till I was forced to do that, at the age of 27 when I joined a job outside my hometown. I had never travelled alone, never taken a bus on my own, never even purchased my own clothing. Everything I needed was taken care of by my parents and the support structure that they had ready for me. I never thought I could have a say in my own life. I was meek, indecisive and confused all at the same time- a recipe for disaster.

Eventually, I rebelled. Because it is crippling, too much love. It is suffocating. It feels like a leash. It leaves too less breathing space for us to grow. It breeds fear, distrust and some degree of lying and manipulating too. I developed a coping mechanism where I didn't have to share everything I did, at home. I found new confidantes. I found solace in books. Sometimes my coping mechanism bordered on escapism.

I once told my therapist (actually just a medical practitioner, I was talking to) that I am indecisive. I don't know what to buy, what to wear, what to eat. I am left flabbergasted when provided with choices. That's the reason I never order at a restaurant. I simply don't know what to pick. I never learned to choose. He simply asked me, "Do you drive?" I said yes I do. "Do you ask the one sitting shotgun where to turn and which route to take to reach your destination?" I said, 'mostly no'. "Then you are not indecisive" he said, " you have to just convert that 'mostly no' to a resounding never".

Simple as that. So I started with the small things, case in point, my new toothpaste. I find a deep seated pleasure, now, in breaking stereotypes, the bigger things, none of that silly toothpaste stuff. I dream of taking it further. Life is too short to be left with regrets at the end.

It is late but it is never too late to evolve, to give oneself a shot at happiness and fulfillment. It's never too late to BE.

Regrets..

June 20, 2017

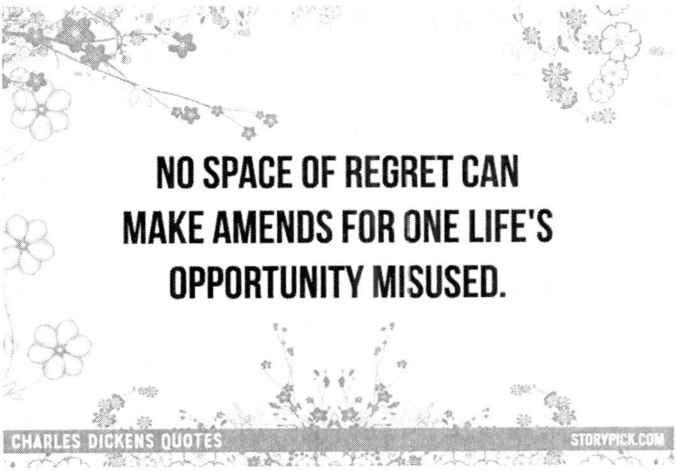

I never thought I would be choosing this title for my blog, EVER because I have always maintained that regrets are such a waste of time and precious energy. In any normal life, people do things which may either work for them or not. But regretting the ones that did not work out has never been my way.

I have always owned my mistakes, learnt from them and moved on. Sometimes, my close ones would agree that, I have been fool enough to repeat some of those mistakes too. But isn't that what life is all about? In my humble opinion, life is a blind deck of experiences. We never know what card will turn up next. We just do the best we can. Sometimes our best sees us through while at other times, we learn.

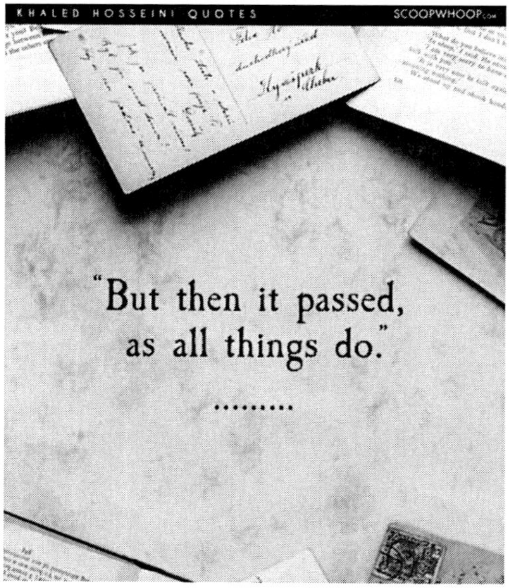

I recently lost my uncle to brain haemorrhage. He was too young to have left us. As the Hindu tradition goes, we were there, paying our tributes and condolences, giving support and strength to the family for twelve solemn days. Even in the midst of all that religious and social bustle, I had a feeling that the real test of strength and perseverance, for the immediate family will begin after the customary rituals got over. After all, they would have to face empty rooms, an empty chair at dinner, the disposing of clothing and other day to day stuff, the inevitable pictures and memories that lie strewn about in any household, even the food would remind them of what he liked best or how much he enjoyed his little indulgences.

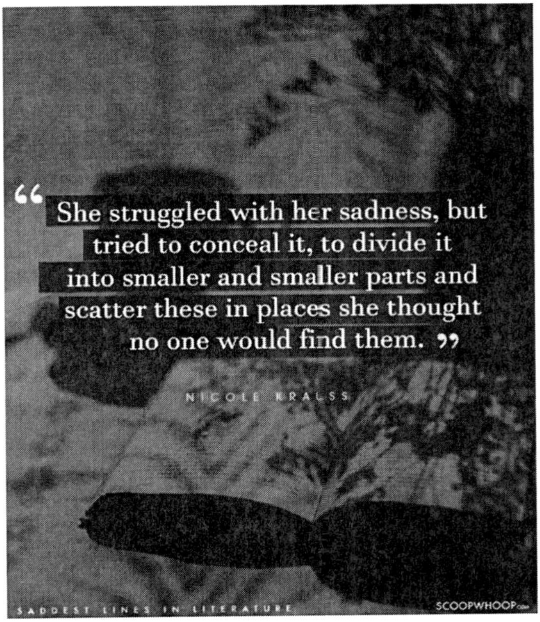

Days have passed and today, as the societal norms dictate, we went to see them all again. To let them know that we are there for them in their hour of need. I learnt a valuable lesson from my grieving aunt because, make no mistake, her grief has just begun. She has a life time of solitude ahead. While recounting some of his last days, my aunt couldn't control her tears and word after word of regret, of unfulfilled dreams, of a life lived in a way that left so much incomplete, so much to want for, poured out of her.

She spelled out the toll that a public life takes on a family. She told us how he was always there for people who approached him for help, how he would ignore his health, his meals, his family for public recognition and to make a name for himself and leave a legacy behind. How he wanted to leave behind his humble beginnings and strained against things that kept him tied down. She told us how that made him irritable and ignited a latent anger in him.

As I sat there listening to her say that "he kept running all his life, we kept fighting- I, to keep him healthy and he to challenge life and destiny despite his health," I couldn't help draw similarities with my own father. He also keeps so much to himself.

I realised what a waste of life and opportunity we all make if we fail to acknowledge and appreciate the people who have always been there for us. In our bid to outdo ourselves, we tend to ignore our closest confidantes, the very people whose unwavering support has been with us throughout our journey. They have stood by us, albeit quietly and may be not in any extraordinary way. They have just been there, believing in us, depending upon us, feeding us when we are hungry, soothing us when we are in a turmoil, laughing with us when we can find no humour in life, sometimes laughing at us when we started to take ourselves too seriously, the ones who kept us grounded. We take them for granted.

If this is not a cause for regret then nothing is. We don't know what tomorrow might bring. We cannot change what happened yesterday but we have complete control on what is happening now. We need to get our priorities right. We need to pay attention. Instead of hurting the people closest to us by our blatant neglect, we should take sometime to recognise their efforts in our life, to be grateful for their presence. Most of all, we should communicate. Yes, speaking up is important. We have to put it all into words, sometimes. We cannot leave things UNSAID, not with people who are so close. True, we understand each other when we are this close, we can interpret each others' silences but it doesn't hurt to say it once in a while.

If we are hurt we should let them know, we should share with them our disappointments- in them, in ourselves or with life, in general. We should let them know if and when we are happy, what act of theirs made us so. Our anger, resentment, grief, pain, should be passed on to them as much as our moments of glory, success, joy & contentment. Sharing a life doesn't just mean living in the same house, providing for each other in the physical or monetary sense alone. It's being there for each other emotionally, that is more important.

Our family, friends, our inner coterie deserve the best part of us. The part which is unspoiled by worldly considerations, the part that is pure and brutally honest. None of us is going to make it out of this life alive. So, let's just make sure that we don't leave any regrets behind. Finding people who genuinely care about and love us, is rare. Let's make it our life's motto to cherish them above all and make our time on this Earth worthwhile because the day we kick the bucket, it's these people in whose hearts we will live forever. Let's give them reasons to love us beyond life & death itself.

Always

June 26, 2017

Our fingerprints do not fade away from the lives we have touched.

Wasn't it J. K. Rowling who made the word ALWAYS mean much more than the Queen's language could ever convey?

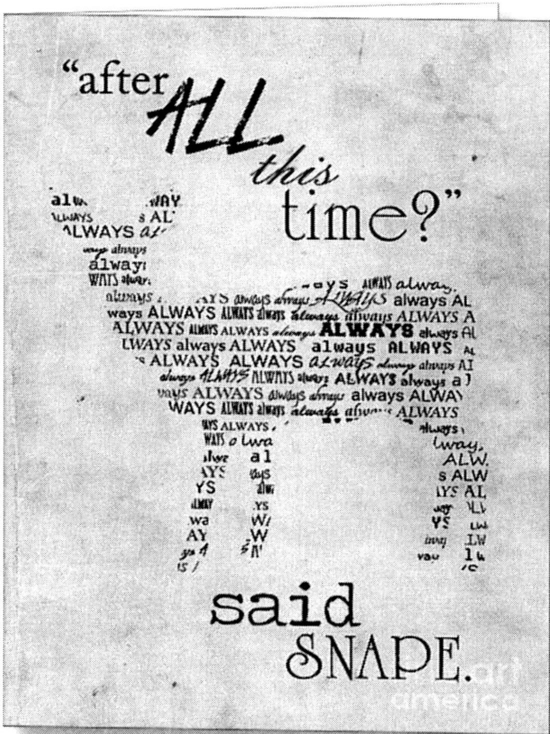

This simple word containing two miniscule syllables came to denote a plethora of emotions. It became a symbol of undying love. It became synonymous with unconditional, unwavering, belief and trust in someone who wasn't even there for you. It escalated the character of Snape from a regular love- jilted villain to a man who didn't want anything in return, a man whose love was never reciprocated, a man who was devoted nevertheless, a man who never gave up, a man who never backtracked on his commitment, whatever the price.

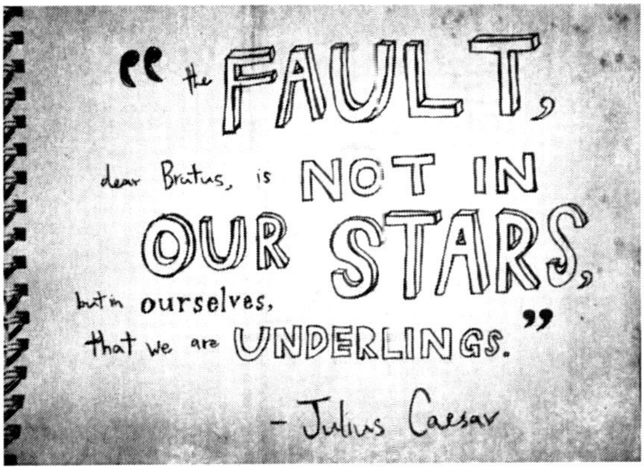

It takes a lot of strength to be that person. It takes a lot of goodness to be able to give out that much love, affection and tenderness. I thought such characters existed only in books. Not getting what one vies for and still making something of one's life, enriching others and still managing to keep that flame burning is Quixotic, it is unreal.

I know a person who has given up everything for the love of his life. His devotion is legendary. His level of commitment, idealistic. He just doesn't know how to give up on her. My piece today salutes him and his spirit. I want to tell him that – it's when you are completely down and out that you get the motivation to rise up again and work for your life. Staying strong and making something of yourself when odds are stacked up against you, proves the mettle of a man.

For me you are the Sun that shines, no matter what. May you get all the happiness in life that you so truly deserve. You embody the word Love. Just direct some of it towards yourself now. I must have done something really good or virtuous to have gotten to know you so closely. Your goodness rubs off on other people. I have been fortunate.

Stay Calm. Stay Strong. Stay the Same. Flourish.

Always.

✨Verbalize the Obvious✨

June 28, 2017

From times immemorial, we have heard this and most of us believe that – "Actions speak louder than words." May be they do but being a logophile myself, I feel words are way important. There is something about words, both written and verbal, that tug at my heart. They don't have to be heavy and impressive all the time. Even the most mundane, regular, unremarkable, simple words, used effectively, do the trick. There is a rhythm to well-strung sentences and phrases. I believe in the beauty of words weaving their magic, their Mystic aura.

Even if I don't talk about the technicality of a well- written piece or a well- expressed speech, I love the way words help us communicate. They bridge the gap better than any other form of communication. I grew up learning that "Speech is Silver while Silence is Golden." As I gained some experience in life, I felt, one needs to speak up, verbalize one's thoughts as much as one can. It clears up the air. It prevents us from ASSUMING the possibilities and makes life a lot easier.

I was going through a Quora thread yesterday and there was a question – Which one line has influenced/ had an impact on you? A very popular Quoran brought up this line that had me thinking. It is so elementary yet honest. The line was- How would you know unless I tell you?

No one can tap into our imagination. Our minds are complex and multi-dimensional. We may be thinking of any particular issue from our point of view, effectively disregarding the view of others. We may believe that we are right and as it, generally, happens in such scenarios, we make up our minds that people around us will react in a certain manner to that particular stimulant. But we will never know, for sure, unless we speak up and share our musings. Things might actually turn out quite the opposite from expectations.

I am not a life guru, far from that actually, I appreciate all the help I can get in leading my life. But there are certain things that I have learnt from experiences. Relationships, for instance, be it with parents, siblings, friends, significant others or people in general. I make it a point to say out loud what I feel for the people in my life. I say – I love you- a lot. EVEN IF IT IS OBVIOUS. Infact, more so when it is obvious. My parents know that I love them, so do my siblings and friends yet I vocalize my emotions, again and again. Some people find it weird. I think it is important. They know what their status in our lives is yet being acknowledged and openly appreciated for always being there, gives them the energy to face their own battles or demons. Who doesn't want to have people looking out for them? I, for one, am extremely grateful and happy when I realise that somebody has my back. So, speaking up, vocalizing, gives further impetus to the one listening. Life remains the same, there is just an added spring in the step when people know that they are adored and valued. A kind word here, a hug there, is all it takes.

How many of us keep it to ourselves when we are upset or disappointed in the people around us? We either yell out our frustration or avoid being in direct line of contact with such people. Meaning, we either vocalize our dissent or make it plain through our actions that we are distressed. We make our feelings known and what a relief it is to have that negativity off of our chests!! Why can't we do the same with positive, life-affirming emotions? Won't that spread a whole lot more joy, happiness, love and understanding in our lives?

I have a motherly figure in my life. I call her Maa. She exemplifies vocalization of the obvious. She is such a charming, generous person. One cannot be anything but full of affection and tenderness around her. I know she loves me and vice versa but she never misses a chance to say so and sometimes that makes all the difference to my dreary day. The good thing is that she balances her words and actions in such a way that whichever philosophy we follow – action or words-we know we are held dear.

Say it if you feel it. Even if it is a tough call, don't worry how people will take it. Being human, each one of us is bestowed with intelligence and emotional quotient to listen, analyse, accept and understand another's point of view. We, eventually, learn to deal with onerous, awkward and irksome matters too. Never hesitate if it is Love you are vocalizing.

Life is short. Don't leave things unsaid.

How would people know unless you tell them?

Think about it.

Prophet's Pearls

June 30, 2017

Today, I just happened to pick a book at random for some quick reading. And what a book it turned out to be!! Every single word, a gem. So, here I am sharing some pearls of wisdom by Kahlil Gibran that he propounds in The Prophet.. The fundamentals never change, do they? They ring as relevant and authentic today, as the day they were written.

On Love

When love beckons to you follow him,

Though his ways are hard and steep.

And when his wings enfold you yield to him,

Though the sword hidden among his pinions may wound you.

And when he speaks to you believe in him,

Though his voice may shatter your dreams as the north wind lays waste the garden.

For even as love crowns you so shall he crucify you. Even as he is for your growth so is he for your pruning.

Even as he ascends to your height and caresses your tenderest branches that quiver in the sun,

So shall he descend to your roots and shake them in their clinging to the earth.

Like sheaves of corn he gathers you unto himself.

He threshes you to make you naked.

He sifts you to free you from your husks.

He grinds you to whiteness.

He kneads you until you are pliant;

And then he assigns you to his sacred fire, that you may become sacred bread for God's sacred feast.

All these things shall love do unto you that you may know the secrets of your heart, and in that knowledge become a fragment of Life's heart.

But if in your fear you would seek only love's peace and love's pleasure,

Then it is better for you that you cover your nakedness and pass out of love's threshing-floor,

Into the seasonless world where you shall laugh, but not all of your laughter, and weep, but not all of your tears.

Love gives naught but itself and takes naught but from itself.

Love possesses not nor would it be possessed;

For love is sufficient unto love.

When you love you should not say, "God is in my heart," but rather, I am in the heart of God."

And think not you can direct the course of love, if it finds you worthy, directs your course.

Love has no other desire but to fulfil itself.

But if you love and must needs have desires, let these be your desires:

To melt and be like a running brook that sings its melody to the night.

To know the pain of too much tenderness.

To be wounded by your own understanding of love;

And to bleed willingly and joyfully.

To wake at dawn with a winged heart and give thanks for another day of loving;

To rest at the noon hour and meditate love's ecstasy;

To return home at eventide with gratitude;

And then to sleep with a prayer for the beloved in your heart and a song of praise upon your lips.

On Marriage

You were born together, and together you shall be forevermore.

You shall be together when white wings of death scatter your days.

Aye, you shall be together even in the silent memory of God.

But let there be spaces in your togetherness,

And let the winds of the heavens dance between you.

Love one another but make not a bond of love:

Let it rather be a moving sea between the shores of your souls.

Fill each other's cup but drink not from one cup.

Give one another of your bread but eat not from the same loaf.

Sing and dance together and be joyous, but let each one of you be alone,

Even as the strings of a lute are alone though they quiver with the same music.

Give your hearts, but not into each other's keeping

For only the hand of Life can contain your hearts.

And stand together, yet not too near together:

For the pillars of the temple stand apart,

And the oak tree and the cypress grow not in each other's shadow.

On Children

Your children are not your children.

They are the sons and daughters of Life's longing for itself.

They come through you but not from you,

And though they are with you, yet they belong not to you.

You may give them your love but not your thoughts.

For they have their own thoughts.

You may house their bodies but not their souls,

For their souls dwell in the house of tomorrow, which you cannot visit, not even in your dreams.

You may strive to be like them, but seek not to make them like you.

For life goes not backward nor tarries with yesterday.

You are the bows from which your children as living arrows are sent forth.

The archer sees the mark upon the path of the infinite, and He bends you with His might that His arrows may go swift and far.

Let your bending in the archer's hand be for gladness;

For even as he loves the arrow that flies, so He loves also the bow that is stable.

On Joy and Sorrow

Your joy is your sorrow unmasked.

And the selfsame well from which your laughter rises was oftentimes filled with your tears.

And how else can it be?

The deeper that sorrow carves into your being, the more joy you can contain.

Is not the cup that hold your wine the very cup that was burned in the potter's oven?

And is not the lute that soothes your spirit, the very wood that was hollowed with knives?

When you are joyous, look deep into your heart and you shall find it is only that which has given you sorrow that is giving you joy.

When you are sorrowful look again in your heart, and you shall see that in truth you are weeping for that which has been your delight.

Some of you say, "Joy is greater than sorrow," and others say, "Nay, sorrow is the greater."

But I say unto you, they are inseparable.

Together they come, and when one sits alone with you at your board, remember that the other is asleep upon your bed.

Verily you are suspended like scales between your sorrow and your joy.

Only when you are empty are you at standstill and balanced.

When the treasure-keeper lifts you to weigh his gold and his silver, needs must your joy or your sorrow rise or fall.

On Reason and Passion

Your soul is oftentimes a battlefield, upon which your reason and your judgment wage war against passion and your appetite.

Would that I could be the peacemaker in your soul, that I might turn the discord and the rivalry of your elements into oneness and melody.

But how shall I, unless you yourselves be also the peacemakers, nay, the lovers of all your elements?

Your reason and your passion are the rudder and the sails of your seafaring soul.

If either your sails or our rudder be broken, you can but toss and drift, or else be held at a standstill in mid-seas.

For reason, ruling alone, is a force confining; and passion, unattended, is a flame that burns to its own destruction.

Therefore let your soul exalt your reason to the height of passion; that it may sing;

And let it direct your passion with reason, that your passion may live through its own daily resurrection, and like the phoenix rise above its own ashes.

I would have you consider your judgment and your appetite even as you would two loved guests in your house.

Surely you would not honour one guest above the other; for he who is more mindful of one loses the love and the faith of both.

Among the hills, when you sit in the cool shade of the white poplars, sharing the peace and serenity of distant fields and meadows – then let your heart say in silence, "God rests in reason."

And when the storm comes, and the mighty wind shakes the forest, and thunder and lightning proclaim the majesty of the sky, – then let your heart say in awe, "God moves in passion."

And since you are a breath In God's sphere, and a leaf in God's forest, you too should rest in reason and move in passion.

On Pain

Your pain is the breaking of the shell that encloses your understanding.

Even as the stone of the fruit must break, that its heart may stand in the sun, so must you know pain.

And could you keep your heart in wonder at the daily miracles of your life, your pain would not seem less wondrous than your joy;

And you would accept the seasons of your heart, even as you have always accepted the seasons that pass over your fields.

And you would watch with serenity through the winters of your grief.

Much of your pain is self-chosen.

It is the bitter potion by which the physician within you heals your sick self.

Therefore trust the physician, and drink his remedy in silence and tranquillity:

For his hand, though heavy and hard, is guided by the tender hand of the Unseen,

And the cup he brings, though it burn your lips, has been fashioned of the clay which the Potter has moistened with His own sacred tears.

👸Lost my Tiara👸

July 2, 2017

I saw an animated episode of the famous Motu Patlu today. These characters were quite famous when we were kids and there was a series of comics of the same name. I remember reading them all. This particular episode I saw, had Motu trying to outrun a pouring cloud. He tried everything in the book and yet couldn't get rid of the cloud. He tried paddling away on a bicycle and the cloud went with him, he disguised himself as a woman to deceive this cloud, that somehow had taken a liking to him, but to no avail. His friend offered him a vaccum cleaner to suck up the cloud, and yet there it was all the more angry and bent on following him. There was no escaping it. It was an animation and hence had to tickle our funny bones. It all actually turned out to be a dream, just the result of his over fertile imagination.

But there are certain things in life that just can't be escaped. Try as we might, we cannot outrun or outsmart them. They are what we call divine providence. Things we have to live with, no matter how.

The circumstances of one's birth is one of those things. We cannot choose who we are born to or who we come out as. Our genders, our race, our family, our position with respect to our siblings, are all things that are beyond our control. Some of these things may turn out to be challenging for us all our adult lives. It wasn't long back that being a woman in India was cause for concern. Women were denied equal rights of life and education. There has been a monumental change in that scenario yet small town India is still not ready to give women their due. It is still an uphill task being a woman here. Even in educated, so called liberal families, the position of the male child is still preferential. The over protective nature of the Indian male, puts an invisible leash on the women of the household. Educated girls are also not supposed to enjoy the same privileges as their brothers. It's debatable, as always has been, that all such steps are necessary for the protection of our women folk, the fairer, weaker sex.

What I can't wrap my head around is the belief that because women marry and leave their parents' home for their marital household, they have no role at all in carrying forward the name of the parents. Even progressive men feel that they should have a male child to further the clan's name and ensure longevity. Where I come from, all virtues of a woman are secondary just because she is a female and all vices of a son are tolerated because he is the one who carries the name of the father. It is hurtful to face this day in and day out. Despite doing everything right, one is still a secondary member of the family. The conservative mindset attached with this social evil is still thriving in our society.

I may be more attuned to the needs and moods of my parents, I may have a better understanding of things around me, a better disposition, a better social circle, a better way of expression, better reasoning and logic, more adaptability, more tolerance, more moral and psychological strength but I am still not good enough. I am not the son. There are things that a daughter is just not capable of. And that makes all the difference.

How I wish, it was a dream, I could evade by waking up just like Motu escaped his dark, angry, pouring cloud!

✨Knead 'em Along✨ Keep'em Close✨

July 7, 2017

As far as household chores are concerned, I particularly pride myself in the kneading of the dough. That was the first thing I learnt and mastered in the kitchen, even before I tried my hand at boiling tea leaves. The process of turning powdery, lacklustre flour into consistent, supple dough, gets me every single time. I am not going to bore you with my culinary expertise 😅 or interests further, instead would get to the point in a jiffy. I am very obsessive about not leaving any trace of flour sticking to the sides of the trough after I am done kneading. I knead and knead and knead till the trough is sparkling clean.

As it always happens when I am a little anxious, my thoughts flow in a rhythm of their own. Things as mundane and unremarkable as kneading dough may also trigger a profound chain of thoughts and emotions. That coupled with anything equally regular may result in a blog like this.

How many people might an average person know at any given point of time? And I am not talking of the thousands that we seem to have on social media accounts. I am talking of people who we meet physically on a daily, fortnightly or monthly basis. Some of whom may be a significant part of our day, others still, also as important and relevant even if we don't see them daily. I have some friends who respond to my good morning messages daily. We may be apart geographically but in that particular instant we are thinking of each other. So, may be a hundred or so people who we are in constant touch with.

Now try and remember how many of them were there when we were growing up or when we were at school or college. The number will dwindle. Rare and special are the people who have the same set of friends and acquaintances in all phases of their lives. As it happens, we fade out of some people's lives and some people fade out of ours. It's a completely natural process. Some go away rather quickly others gradually. The ones that just move along as our lives take us places, are the ones that don't hurt. We treasure the memories they left us with, without even realising that they are hidden someplace inside the maze, our minds are. Someday we come across an old letter or photograph of them or we reconnect via Facebook and voila, the slideshow of memories begin!

This happened with me today. I reconnected with an elder didi of mine who also happened to have taught me once, long back, and I couldn't hold back memories. She was the first person I had heard speaking, effortlessly, in English. She had a beautiful handwriting. Some phrases that I picked up while she taught us English and History, have remained with me ever since. I realised that everytime I have ever used those phrases, I have fondly remembered her. It had become so much a habit with me that my mind could never erase the mental picture of her I carried. Her face had not faded away like it happens with people who drift apart. I perused her profile and found that after so many years she still looks the same – well turned out, smiling, wise eyes, an air of intellect surrounding her that is not limited by the fact that I just saw a picture of her. Though short in stature, her personality looms large for me. I cherish what she gave me as a child. I was at an impressionable age and I am glad that I got to learn from her. I hold dear, her contribution in shaping me, however little it may seem. It is immensely significant for me. Indelible!! It's true, we never realise how much space we take up in other people's lives and minds.

At times I am a little anxious of talking to people from my own past because try as they might people do change and I am afraid that the mental image I carry inside may not match with the stark reality of what time and space have turned them into. Nevertheless, it is still mighty fabulous to be able to recall so much of our past and people's role in it, frame by frame. It's a heady feeling to agnise that just like footprints on the moon, certain marks always remain, clear and incorruptible.

It is a whole other story with the people we have to leave after a falling out of ways. They are the ones who stay the longest in our minds and hearts. Always at the forefront! They are like the hint of flour left on the sides and base of the trough after the kneading is done. We so want them to be a part of our dough, our life but as it happens with dough, so it is in life. We cannot accomplish the desired inclusion without tempering with the consistency of either. I hate leaving people behind, I would rather disrupt the harmony or regularity of my life than to let go of people that, once, enriched it. But all of us have to take tough decisions at times and that is where the anxiety creeps in. Anyone who leaves, takes a part of us with them. True, we adapt, but we are never the same again.

How I wish that keeping people close were a skill to be mastered, like kneading! I could have learnt that and would have never left anyone behind. EVER.

Recipe for Respite

July 16, 2017

It was my first job, teaching at my mother's school. There was a cultural function just round the corner and while making a model for the exhibition or a prop for the stage, I don't remember which, I had fallen short of adhesive and a colleague of mine had offered me some araldite, which they were using for some woodwork. He had playfully mimed its advertisement, Araldite – sticks everything except broken hearts. Since then, I always think of this punchline and the product when I find things broken.

Time has flown by since those green years. A late bloomer, I had no use of advice on broken hearts till quite late in my life. By then I had developed my own coping mechanism. I had found solace in the written word. I found peace, quiet and a deep sense of calm in music. A book could cure me of anything that ailed me. So could music.

When things got a bit more messy, I discovered F. R. I. E. N. D. S, the TV show. No matter what I was feeling, however low, anxious or broken, I could watch it and relieve my inner turbulence.

I have grown since then too. I have realised that escapism of this kind, distractions of these sort have a limited shelf life. It's not until we face our demons, look them in the eye, think, analyse, accept and come to conclusions, that we find peace within. No person, worth his or her salt, who has ever lived, can escape the challenges that life poses and we grow only when we take them on fearlessly, with an open mind and heart.

I have recently discovered an ultimate Recipe for Respite – Cooking. It's something that has kept women going, for ages. It's what has kept them together. I am thirty seven, and for the first three decades of my life I had no or minimum concern with household chores, no cooking, no cleaning, no house keeping for me. I would instead read. That is the luxury of an extremely efficient elder sister and a doting younger one. Between them, they had the kitchen and household covered.

I never thought I would ever say that, much less write about it but the kitchen has now become my sanctuary. Whatever my mood, it can be lifted just by being there on my own for an hour or two. In a household full of people and voices, it sometimes become difficult to hear you own self. Cooking gives me that, much needed, opportunity to shut out all other voices and just have a conversation with myself. It's the most precious ME time I get. Many of my blogs have been thought and conceptualised while Chopping, Grating, Kneading or Peeling.

Even if I do no thinking while cooking a dish, I end up feeling cleansed, serene and calm once I am through. It gives me immense satisfaction to think up new ways of making the same old veggies. It invigorates my mind, body and soul. I have experienced that cooking not only rejuvenates my mind, detoxing me of stress and anxiety but also relieves me of aches and physical discomfort. The sheer pleasure of making something while I can think and analyse 'N' number of topics, is refreshing and comforting.

It's the place where I, Saute my Stress, Chop at Concerns, Grate Grief, Knead away Knots, Fry the Fears, Boil Boredom, Grill Grudges, Peel Pressures, Wash away Worries, Trundle Trepeditions, Cube the Qualms, Marinate Malice and Malevolence, Bake Benevolence, Chill Certainty, Ladle my mind into a Lull and finally Dish out Determination.

And the best part is, I try not to avoid my apprehensions, instead I confront them, deal with them as best as I can, accept and move on.

I am suddenly out of words so I am gonna give it a rest, until next time.

To Neha, with Love 😘

July 18, 2017

I don't exactly remember the day I first met you. I have a vague recollection that I saw you first in Hostel 2s3 where you and your friends were working on a chart of toppers in the warden's room and I, a new appointee, was asked to oversee the task. I didn't do much of overseeing, just looked over the language and observed the 'rowdiest group on the campus' work with a nonchalance which I was far from feeling. It was in my second year as a teacher there, that I was asked to take your class. All sorts of horror stories were attached with Class X- A. I was told that I would be booed out of the class if I am lucky, if not, I could face cat calls, indiscriminate hooting or even a chalk missile from even the most innocent looking girl, while I was writing on the blackboard.

Mercifully, none of that happened. What transpired was an instant connection with the entire class. Contrary to popular belief, I had never come across a group of girls so eager to learn. It was the quietest, most disciplined class ever. I remember, vividly, the Sunday extra classes too which you all attended with such gusto. Teaching history has never been more fun than with my Class X-A. I remember pretty much everyone from that room but the ones who have stayed beyond that classroom, beyond school, are few. You and Chhavi, the dearest among them.

When I look back, I can't pinpoint the exact moment, we started talking but somehow, by God's grace, I found your little group full of potential, only the veneer of mischief and recklessness needed to be peeled off.

I am sure you remember the unfortunate incident that happened when you were in Hostel 3s2 and I was off for an exam. Once that happened, I wanted to see you win at all costs. By winning I don't mean the argument or the strife, I mean to make it big in life. I dreamt that you all, closest to my heart, would take a turn for the better, write a new page and be exemplary scholars and achievers.

Neha, you have made all of us very proud by adding feather after feather in your beautifully adorned cap. The best thing about you is that success sits so lightly on your shoulders. You have managed to stay humble and grounded even after the accolades that have come your way.

For me, you are already a ✵ that brightens my horizon. I recall your lament when you could not make it to the roll of honors but surely you too must realise now that, it was just a minor set back in the bigger scheme that God had for you.

Being meritorious all your life, you further proved your worth by coming out, unscathed if a little scratched, of the many tight corners that life has thrown your way. You made loss your strength and fulfilled the dream of your father, against all odds.

Today, I am proud not just because your perseverance has paid off and you have accomplished the goal of becoming a Chartered Accountant, I am proud of the person you have become. I am amazed by the sheer strength of your will, your humility and the grace that you have acquired along the way.

Do you know what your name means? It means love, friendship, one who is adored, the eyes that see, the innocent dew that laces the surface at dawn. You are amongst the rare few who personify the very traits of their name.

I am out of words for the emotions that are running pell-mell in my mind. I just want to Congratulate you on your achievement and for bringing so much happiness to all those who love you.

Stay humble. Stay the same. Keep Smiling. Keep Winning.

Love Always,

Lubhita

✨Memory✨

July 31, 2017

It is in the Music that lies forgotten in my soul,

It erupts in the Moody rhythm of my dejected heart,

It lies in the Musings of my Muddled Mind,

It reverberates in the empty Minutes of the hours we talked for,

It finds voice in my Melancholic words,

It echoes in the word 'Maa' you so lovingly called me.

Alas, with you gone, your Memory is everywhere!

I didn't realize what I was missing till you came along.. Now that you are gone, the vacuum is intimidating, the silence deafening.. I miss you.

💔Yearning Heart💔

August 15, 2017

How the Heart Yearns!
For things that are beyond our reach.
The notions that the elders never preach.
For love, friendship and relations that instigate,
our very souls, against what the world propagates.
For chances & opportunities that are on the take
but for the leashes, we could make.
We do what is expected of us,
for family- society, the whole corpus.
We yen, we ache, we pine, we languish.
And our hearts yearn for something to accomplish,
something to Cherish!!
Ah, What Anguish!!!

Utopian Realities

August 29, 2017

I had heard people speak about it and I am sure I also must have, at some point in my teaching career, provided lip service to the sentiment of 'following one' s heart' or 'doing what one is passionate about'. I have examples galore of the fact that people do give up on their dreams when life happens. The race to earn and accumulate wealth to support a desired lifestyle or to provide for a family takes prominence in the larger scheme of things. An extremely gifted writer friend of mine, Prerak, muses thus-

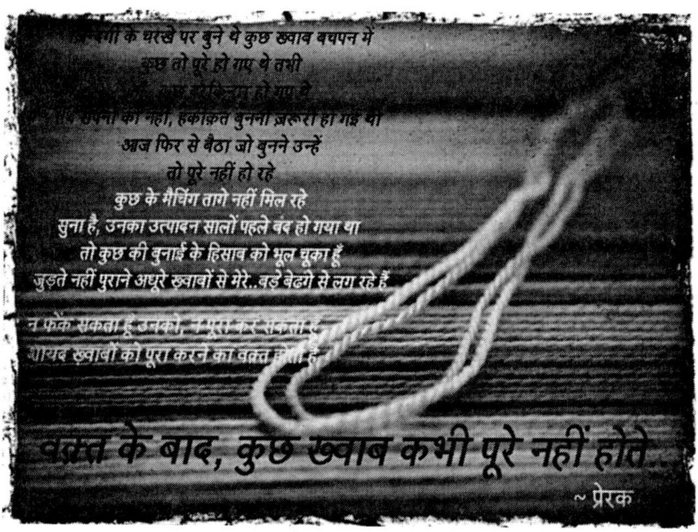

Our passions and interests take a back seat. Things that once gave us immense pleasure or those that brought out our creativity and latent instincts are all but lost. True, the flame doesn't extinguish completely but the heat is gone. We tend to take them up as hobbies and then we write, paint, sing, dance, cook or travel when time and circumstances permit.

Few amongst us have the fortune of really doing what we were cut out for. And such people shine through any crowd. They have their life sorted out at least in the way they want to lead it. They are not compromising on their dreams and thus their work speaks. There is a special aura around them that attracts people wherever they go. And some of it rubs off on people like us, with association. The past couple of months have been one such mystical journey for me, thanks to such charming friends who simply love what they do and are eager to share their exploits or take us along where their Vagrant Minds or Itchy Feet take them.

She defines Art as the medium of the creative & Artists, for her, are people who have the vision to see beyond the obvious. In no way she believes Art to be elitist.. Meet Dr. Sangeeta Singh, artist par excellence, creating waves on the Jaipur Art Scene for years now. Her brand of Art is inclusive of the laymen. To her, Art is finding a charm and beauty in the mundane, everyday things.. It's one's perspective that gives a different meaning and scope to things that are otherwise unremarkable or ordinary.. Come to think of it, even ordinary is art..

I have had the distinct pleasure of knowing her for a decade now and in all these years I have seen her grow as an artist. I am an ignoramus when it comes to art so much so that I can't even draw a leaf to save my life but she never looked down upon me. Working together, once we had to make some invitation cards. She had an abstract concept of shades and strokes and weird eye catching combinations that gave life to those cards. What is significant is that she didn't do it by herself, she motivated us to participate. What fun we had! Added to it was the satisfaction of having made them ourselves. That was, some eight years back.

I was recently invited to one of her Art Exhibitions that she had put up at the Kalaneri Art Gallery, Jaipur, in collaboration with numerous other artists and students of Art. Having missed out on a couple of her previous exhibitions in as many years, I decided to visit this one, come what may. It turned out to be a sound decision on my part.

The central theme of the exhibition was to create best out of waste. Her corner, according to me, was the most creative and interactive. And I am not saying that because of my long standing association with the artist but because her passion for her work was evident even to an unskilled eye and mind like me. Her vision was not just for what is, but also for what can be and what should be!

She had a female mannequin buried in a huge wooden crate filled with sand, depicting Mother Earth with blue ribbons running out of her hands, depicting the flowing water or rivers. Her message of sustainable development wasn't lost on anyone who cared to wander in. With one stroke of genius, one little corner in the exhibition room, she not only underlined the reckless and brutal misuse of earth's resources by Man but also the need to conserve them – our forests and water.

Her blue line (ribbon) symbolically flowed out of the hands of Mother Earth, climbed up the steps of the gallery and continued to flow beyond the premises. She made sure that the guests understood her idea and participated in it by planting little saplings along her blue line. Her acute sense of Art and spirited presentation of this seemingly ordinary concept, was extremely impressive & remarkable. We left the venue, enriched and happy to have shown our solidarity with this grave issue in such an artistic yet simplistic way.

Sangy has moved on to yet another venture. She is putting up her work for the Delhi people too. She recently had an inauguration at ITC Sheraton, as part of Classique.

May she have further hues to add to her already vivid, vibrant montage of life.

Another, much younger inspiration came to me from an ex-student of mine who has now made a name for himself as a web designer, photographer & a cinematographer with sharp skills & a keen eye for details.

Sourabh Gaur, hails from the sleepy town that is Bikaner yet he didn't let his dream die. His aspirations became his motivation and as they say no hurdle is big enough for a sentient mind and a willing heart. He set out to scale a mountain – both literally and figuratively.

In the picturesque locales of Himachal, the peak he aimed at, stood some 18,750 feet high. To reach the acme, was going to be a test of one's grit and determination. He tread, on foot, the path deemed too risky for nimble footed animals too. His eyes open only to the Vivid Vistas stretched out before him.

So complete was his will to be one with nature that he ignored the risk and just concentrated on the goal and along the way made good use of the journey itself. He chose to look at the ethereal skies, verdant vales, lofty peaks & the beauty that lay beyond the rough, slippery terrain. And how true the words ring- The best views come after the hardest climb.

His pictures are proof enough of the exciting trek he embarked upon. He is reluctant to share the details & the location of his adventure because he feels that the pristine, almost virginal peace & beauty of that place wouldn't remain intact if more people knew about it.

Yet another venture that makes one believe that our future is in safe, responsible hands, is the Bikaner City Blog.

Aimed at promoting and nurturing the culture, history, food, lifestyle & young talent of the city, this non profit organization is run by highly motivated youngsters fresh out of colleges. They organise events to popularise the legacy and inheritance of our colorful yet quiet city.

They are working hard to provide a platform to the youth of the city to showcase their passions and talents. In the same spirit, they organised a Musical Meet a couple of days back. I couldn't make it to the event but saw live updates on various social media platforms that have knit our lives so closely together, and once again I was in awe of these nestlings that are so eager to give wings to their imagination.

The meet, first of its kind in our city, was a resounding success. It was heartening to witness Art in such raw, pure, unadulterated form. The satisfaction and bliss of following one's own heart was written large on the smiling, shiny faces and in the sparkling, expectant eyes of the performers. They sang and played their hearts out.

A group of three friends got together to begin the Golden Sand Production Company that is fast becoming a household name in our torpid little town. Away from the humdrum & glamour of big cities, ours is a laid back society that is nevertheless rich in tastes and talents. The idea behind Golden Sands is to bring forth the vivacious, lesser known facts about our city, to acquaint the people, young and old, with the eccentricities and idiosyncratic tendencies of our Bikaner. They churn out music videos, promote acting and dramatic talents, organise events, and take up socially responsible tasks in their bid to fulfill their dreams.

It is not as if these are the first amongst us to break away from a well – paved path to attain what their hearts really desire, neither will they be the last. But wherever they feature in the hierarchy, they are worth a mention because they are doing what they do best. They have digressed from the prescribed and recommended courses to carve out their own. They took a risk to dive head along in the labyrinth of life and have come out tops.

People who do what they are destined to do, are a different breed altogether. They don't shy away from the challenges that life, inevitably, throws their way. Nothing can stop them from pursuing their cherished fantasies. Their simple charm in being what they truly are, cannot be hidden, anywhere they go and whatever crowd they mingle in. There is no mediocrity in the work they undertake. They stand out as resplendent representatives of mankind.

When they write, it is Lyrical. When they paint, it is Sublime. When they sing, it is Soulful. When they dance, it is Synchronic. When they cook, it is Heavenly. When they travel, it is to explore the Unknown. When they pick up the camera, it is to capture Glory. When they create, it is Magic!!

⏳Borrowed Minutes⏳

September 3, 2017

Ah! The grave anguish
Of meeting you again,
The mixed feelings of being with you,
the longing, the pain.
It has been a year,
we had that row.
And parted ways,
tried to let go..
Things didn't work out
as I envisaged.
It's probable, I am getting
difficult with age.
Don't get me wrong,
I love to see you flourish.
Your triumphs, your laughter,
Your memories I cherish.
You flit in and out of my life.
This is your right.
Yet, fleeting is your attention,
blind, the sight.
The scant time you can accord

leads me to believe,
I won't pass away with a regret,
the bond we forged will provide reprieve.
Overwhelmed with love and joy
of your company, I forgo the claim.
But do tell me if I deserve just
these Borrowed Minutes to my name..

Fare thee Well!

September 14, 2017

Crumbling Consanguinity

September 18, 2017

There is this advertisement doing the rounds on television these days. It's about home loans being offered by a bank. What I like about the ad is its story and concept.

It shows a well educated mother – son duo, in all probability living in a metropolis, discussing the concept of having separate living solutions once the son gets married. She tells him to listen to her and get a place of his own, somewhere nearby, to avoid unpleasantness & tough choices, between mother and wife, in future. The son is bewildered at the thought of living away from his mother but out of confusion dawns comprehension of what she is trying to explain to him in such a matter of fact way.

The emotional ebb & flow giving way to relief and a solid decision, is evident on his face. What appeals to me is – first, the mother in the driving seat, both literally and figuratively. Second, her profound wisdom & deep rooted understanding of the way things are in families these days and the ease with which she imparts that to her son. Third, and most important, we see a parent, a mom, relinquishing control over the offspring, in an effort to keep him close.

Not very long ago, the Indian family system was unique in the world. We were the benchmark with which the world compared & learnt of filial duty & responsibility. I am sure all of us in the late thirties or forties have heard our parents go on and on about living in a joint family. How the patriarch, or in some cases the matriarch, of the family presided over the lives and decisions of all the members. How elders were free to correct the conduct of any child in the family.

How meals were always a time to come together & rejoice. How similar opportunities of education and jobs were open to every child in the family. Family picnics and outings did not need to be arranged over the phone. Any one of the elders could take all the kids out to a movie or picnic. They stayed together, ate together, travelled together.. In essence, their lives were intertwined with each other so much, that the concept of cousins or half siblings was lost on them. They were all brothers and sisters. Their parentage, their identity was not confined to their sets of parents, it encompassed the entire family.

Where on the one hand, parents or the elders, came to expect a certain conduct and attitude from the children of their family, on the other, children too relied heavily on the decisions of their elders. Married or not, every young person had to conform to the ways of the family. Even new brides got to learn anew and adjust their upbringing and disposition according to the family they were married into. The basic principles of being respectful towards all, remained unchanged.

Sadly, what we see around us these days is something completely different. What we see are ruins of the old family system. Gone are the joint families and the way they nurtured lives within, the way they passed on the legacy. No longer are elders free to point out misconduct or mistakes of the young who are not their sons or daughters by the privilege of birth, in some cases even that is not possible. Brides these days prefer to stay nuclear. They prefer to look after their husbands and kids and don't want to be burdened with the complications of an extended family. Parents-in-law, brothers-in-law, sisters -in-law, remain just that- in laws.. They don't become a part of their families.

We take it in our stride and move on, accepting it as the need of the hour or something that is happening with everyone these days. Not all families or elders are as eager as the mother in the ad, to let go of their children to make a family or a life of their own. Most parents tend to stay on even in adverse circumstances. I have witnessed sons and their wives throwing abuse after abuse at these aging parents. Nothing they do, seem to the young as coming from good intentions or a sense of love and responsibility towards their children and grand children. The same son who was lovingly and so painstakingly brought up by them, turns on them as soon as he gets a wife.The children of the family suffer the most. Their childhood is scarred and their lives shape up witnessing the strifes between their parents and grandparents.

Resultantly, there are either sob stories to tell if the parents decide to stay home & deal with insult after insult hurled at them or old age homes filled to the seams.

Neither case resembles the old glory of the family system that we were so proud of.

We talk of western influence in such derogatory terms most of the time but I feel their family system is much more sorted than ours. They have accepted that once a child starts earning or going out in society, his/her identity as their child alone, ceases to exist. They become their own people, capable of taking important decisions of their lives and dealing with the repercussions. They know that parents can guide them but can't protect them forever. They understand the need of letting their children be. They may not turn out exactly as their parents want them to but they are happy and satisfied because they become what they are, on their own steam. Staying separate does not come after marriage. It comes as soon as the child starts to earn a living. The love and affection that they have for their elders is not feigned because the constant bickering and nagging is absent from their daily lives.

I am a complete sucker for joint family systems but with the way things are these days it is infinitely better to follow the west and live with respect than to stick with what is expected as a societal obligation and stay unhappy. This holds true & goes both for parents and kids..

Just a random thought.. Would love to have your views.

👼The Way I Am👸

September 22, 2017

"There will come a day when you will realise what you actually want. Your search will end, it will reach its culmination and that would be the day you probably would stop reading and writing. Whatever you write thereafter will be a complete thought. Your words will want for nothing. You will have achieved what your soul is so desperately looking for in the written word," so saying, he smiled enigmatically.

"But, I don't think I am looking for anything in particular. I read because I love to and I write only when I have things to say. Yes, sometimes, I have incomplete thoughts that might need processing. Sometimes, I write things that are raw. I write of emotions, of people, of love, of loss. I write of things that are human. I read things that I find fun or that stir me. I have never thought of reading as a channel to get somewhere, it has never been purpose oriented, merely a means of getting to know stuff," I riposted.

"Ah! But you are young still, you will get there, eventually," he reiterated.

What is it about thinking individuals that ruffles our set opinions so? It isn't as if I change my thought process on every word of a book or a firmly stated opinion but both mediums compel me to re-analyse my approach. Sometimes I defer to the books or educated opinions thrown at me, at others I stick with whatever wisdom I have acquired over the years.

I maintain that I don't read with a purpose in mind. I am neither spiritual nor religious enough to seek answers in mythological text, I am not condemning them or denying their significance, it's just that they don't work for me as well as a fictional work with deep rooted meaning does. I would rather read a Shantaram or To kill a mockingbird or Rumi, even for that matter a Brida, to get perspective on life, than to look for solutions in the Bhagwad Gita. I have read that too but probably I did not get it much.

I started writing as a catharsis for my broken spirit. I never felt that my pieces had or have any literary merit. I write because, there comes a time in each of our lives when we have things to say that we can't express freely, even to the closest of our friends or family. Some keep it all bottled up or lock it all up in the deepest recesses of their minds, some choose art, music, cooking, travelling, gardening, keeping pets, chatting or even socialising to keep that inner voice down. To each his or her own.

I Choose to Write. I can't, at times, express what I am going through even with my writings, for fear of being judged. I still haven't learnt how to fictionalize my accounts so that I am finally able to pour my heart out without anyone finding out the trials I am going through. I, forever, dread the query, who is it you have written about in this piece?

Still, I choose to write to attain temporary relief, a sense of calm from my ever accumulating thoughts. I may stop writing if by some miracle I can stop thinking of mundane, everyday things. I am an ordinary being, a human with trappings like love, desires, wishes, hopes, friendships & relationships. I don't see myself graduating to the bigger questions of life and existence any time soon.

May be, I am missing an essential ingredient. It is probable that I am lost. I may not conform to many things that this world lays down but I am ME. I will own up to my mistakes, I am the one who would take lessons from them. I might repeat some of them but I am content. My energy is my own. I regret nothing. Even bad decisions and failures were necessary. They probably were the most important things in my life when they happened.

I am here to lead a simple, uncomplicated, knowledge – centric life and I feel that I am on my way pretty much the way I wanted to be. I love to wear my heart on my sleeve and won't apologise for being the way I am.

Freedom at Midnight

October 2, 2017

Turning the final pages of Freedom at Midnight, I couldn't help but marvel at the skill, sorcery & verve of these two master story tellers- Dominique Lapierre and Larry Collins.

I had read 'Is Paris burning?' by the same authors some years back and that still remains one of my favorite books on the Holocaust. But I always maintained that writing about one's own country or region, researching the history, events and facts about it is a lot easier, less stringent, hence the flow of writing. Dominique Lapierre is a Frenchman himself, so probably that's the reason the book turned out the way it did.

But "Freedom at Midnight" opened my eyes to the magic of their words. Right from the first page, one is absorbed in the narrative. The exhaustive research is evident in the minor details of the events that shaped History.

Partition of India and the communal tension that resulted is a hugely sensitive topic and yet they have told the story as History needs to be told. Their non~partisan attitude brings a crispness to the narrative which is so many times missing from Historical commentaries.

Finishing the book, a reader is free to choose his or her own hero. The writers have not been partial to any one character.

They have been honest and sincere. They have written things and drawn out characters as they understood them.

If one is a Gandhian by principle,they will find that Gandhi is, infact, the hero here. If one has rightist inclinations, they will have Veer Savarkar, Narayan Apte, Nathuram Godse and their ilk to fawn upon. And if one believes in the contributions and impact of the British then they will have the Mountbattens to look up to after going through this book.

The authors have not colored their text with their own judgement on Indian history and its major players. It is for each of us to read and make out which YugPurush to idolize.

They have steered clear of any controversy by avoiding a major pitfall that all history authors face~ they haven't caricaturised any of the political leaders of the time. They have been equally indifferent to Jinnah, Nehru or Patel. While they make it a point to mention them wherever necessary, these leaders are not the core around which their book spins.

These two are men on a mission. Their mission being~ to relate the story of the Indian Independence, Partition & the biggest exodus that the world has ever witnessed. The events leading up to 15th August 1947, the common people who faced the brunt of partition, the senseless killings, the loss of men & property, the challenges of these newly formed nations, the role of the parting British, the steadfastness of the Mahatma, his ultimate sacrifice for his people, the masses, the teeming millions of India, thus divided, are the real protagonists of their narrative. Riveting!! All 750 plus pages of it!!! Please get your copies now!!

I, myself, have been a history student for years now and I have always avoided being labeled a secular or a Gandhian or leftist or rightist. But one cannot remain unmoved & undecided after reading this book and I have come out strongly in favor of the Mahatma after going through the text. It, so often, happens in the history of civilizations that we crucify our Gods & Messiahs while they are living and build temples in their names once they are gone.

Nearly 70 years since his death, Gandhi and his principles have seen every reaction that is possible for a multitude to give. He was revered in his lifetime and equally hated in the aftermath of partition. He realised in the last years of his life, the futility of his methods in a newly independent nation. He saw his friends and protégé moving away from the ideals that had won them this precious Freedom. There was a surge in his popularity once more when he passed away. Years have passed since then. We have limited him to text books, postal stamps or currency notes. His principles, once the guiding beacons of hope to millions, have now been rendered obsolete. There comes a time in the history of every nation when they pay lip service to their greats. We have done that to the Mahatma. It is disheartening to see students and even older people criticise him for what he never was or never did. It breaks my heart to see people shrugging his contributions off or comparing his role in Indian independence with militant leaders or revolutionaries, to ultimately find him wanting.

Gandhi knew that history won't be kind to him. He knew how the minds of his people worked. He had one thumb firmly planted on the nerve of India. He realised that the next generation might not accord him a position of respect when talking of the Indian Independence struggle. He knew but he didn't care. He was perseverant right till his last breath. When told by a refugee to leave the Indian people alone and go to the Himalayas for his remaining days, Gandhi said, "This is my Himalaya", referring to the post independence communal turmoil. He lived for the nation and he died for it. He knew no other way to live.

The light truly went out of our lives when he was assassinated but his light shines through, even now, for those who are willing to open their eyes and minds to see, learn & understand.

We, as a nation, should be grateful that he was born here and lived amongst us.

The Move

November 2, 2017

For as long as I can remember, I wanted to move back to the city. It wasn't that I loved my home any less but to live away from society is a challenge in its entirety. There are daily struggles that one has to go through even to maintain the home and hearth. After quite a lot of deliberation and cajoling we succeeded in convincing our parents to give up their recluse-like lifestyle and return to the city. For twenty- two long years, they had been dwelling at the farm. It was home, it still is.

After looking for it high and low, we finally settled for this new place – a penthouse apartment that accorded my parents their much- needed space in addition to being a lot more convenient to us. We gradually started visualizing the home that it would turn into. All efforts went into making it the space that all of us dreamt of.

Moving in, though demanding & stressful, was the easy part. What we feared, were apprehensive about, but at the same time looked forward to, was getting used to the people, the newness of being around a lot of people, of dealing with them on a daily basis. I was wary of my social skills, for one. Having stayed away for such a long time might have rusted whatever little people skills I had, to start with.

The people in our building all looked happy and welcoming yet there was a sort of breaking (back) – in required. We got the perfect opportunity to meet and greet and test our social skills outside our immediate community when we were invited by new flat owners moving into the building, just a fortnight after us.

It was a pleasant experience and everybody seemed to genuinely like and respect each other. I had heard my mother speak about neighbours being more family than families ever are but it was the first experience of the sort. Ours being a new apartment building, we were all trying to get to know each other but there was an openness, a comfort, a will to establish and build up new acquaintances.

There are so many aspects to moving in and settling down. Not only does one need to get used to the novelty of the new abode and its surroundings but one also has to adjust to the unbeaten and untrodden schedules and paths that lie waiting.

It is a happy coincidence then, that our move is working well for nearly all of us. The freshness of the routine, the zest to face each day that brings with it disparate experiences, recommencing the activeness that life was just a couple of decades ago, recapturing the beauty and essence of city life once again, are all things that we hoped for.

What the Move has made me realise is that deep down, under the veneer that we had on for twenty odd years, we are all people's persons. There is a profound and unfeigned affection for people that runs right beneath the parched stratum of our personalities.

I hope the move does us good. Looking forward to many happy and content years here. May these be the verdant grounds where new and everlasting memories take root..

Grace changes Everything

November 14, 2017

Just this morning, while surfing the internet in my customary fashion, I came across the definition of the word Nostalgia.

Having used the word to great effect over the years, it didn't seem quite extraordinary, specially when I read it for the first time. But as they say, some things are better understood when felt, words just can't do justice to them.

At 37, I have been lucky to experience various facets of life- its triumphs, its joys, the memories of togetherness, friendships, relations, and simultaneously and very obviously- the trials, the tough times, the breakups, the leaving behind of places and people.

Every 'rich' life has its ups and downs. The mind, invariably, misses and remembers moments of glee and grief alike. There are triggers that set off the flow of memories and emotional people, like me, love to delve into them, relive them, sometimes to my own chagrin.

I am not a methodical writer, never have been. If I deliberately try to pen down something, it comes through as an invested effort, which is fake, at worst and dishonest, at best. My words flow only when they are inspired by something or someone. I am a handicap that way. That's the reason I am so irregular in my posts. The daily nitty-gritty of life, the mundane blandness of living, hardly give us reasons to invest into words. It's only when a memory strikes and I long to go back into time to experience, once again, the joy of that moment or to freeze it so that it can be a physical part of me, that I write.

For days now, I had been lamenting the fact that I wasn't able to create anything. Granted, I have been busy but isn't writing or creation something that we do to feed our Souls not to fill our pockets? Time or lack of it should, then, not be an impediment.

My current move to the city fills me with so many new experiences every single day. Be it the presence of people around or the cacophony of traffic, the blaring loudspeakers belting out song after song celebrating weddings or religious ceremonies. The lights, the sounds, the sights – every little thing fills me with wonder. Try as I might, I can't write about them. Or atleast I can't start with writing about them. It's only things that I long for, things that have come to pass for better or for worse, that stir up my imagination.

I saw a familiar face today. Someone I had had to leave behind, not on very good terms too. Miraculously, I couldn't remember anything bad about our association even when I happened to glance at him. True, there was a longing to shout out for attention but good sense prevailed and there & then the realisation of moving on struck me. I have already accepted the turn of events. I am aware that self respect and happiness are the most important ingredients of a fulfilling life and that some people are meant to meet us only to give us this lesson, they are there merely to make us understand what we don't need in our lives.

We are life long learners, the human race. Too much information, too many words, too large an exposure to recorded and written life- lessons make us immune to them. After a while we stop sorting & sifting through them, a perfunctory read is all we accord them. Doesn't it happen with too many text messages or motivational quotes that we come across on social networking sites? We read them, if we have to, but reading is far from assimilation. It's only when we endure a certain situation or come face to face with reality, that we learn. And as I said, we learn everyday, even without books, without quotes, without religious, inspirational or motivational communes. Life is a hard task master. It has its exclusive way of getting through to us.

All I have learnt in recent years is that Self – love is important. Self-respect is an integral part of it. Someone who cannot respect us, isn't fit to be loved by us. If we don't love ourselves, we cannot channel that love outside, towards someone else. It isn't selfish to put ourselves first. It is a prerequisite for sound mental health and eventually, one's physical, social & psychological well being too.

I am grateful today that I got this life and that I have lived it the way I have. There are so many things to be thankful for, so many people that form the crux of my being, myriad events that shaped me into the person I am today. There is no place for Regrets. What and whoever is present, is the best that has happened to me. Whatever existed fleetingly, enriched me with experiences.

So, while the event that sparked off this train of thoughts might be intense nostalgia or a very strong memory, it surely isn't Regret and what it definitely is, is Grace.

And, Grace changes Everything.

Through the Looking Glass

November 19, 2017

A seagull was flying over a beach, when it saw a mouse. It flew down and asked the mouse:

"Where are your wings?"

Each animal speaks its own language, and so the mouse didn't understand the question, but stared at the two strange, large things attached to the other creature's body.

"It must have some illness," thought the mouse.

The seagull noticed the mouse staring at its wings and thought:

"Poor thing. It must have been attacked by monsters that left it deaf and took away its wings."

Feeling sorry for the mouse, the seagull picked it up in its beak and took it for a ride in the skies. "It's probably homesick," the seagull thought while they were flying. Then, very carefully, it deposited the mouse once more on the ground.

For some months afterward, the mouse was sunk in gloom; it had known the heights and seen a vast and beautiful world. However, in time, it grew accustomed to being just a mouse again and came to believe that the miracle that had occurred in its life was nothing but a dream.

I was reading 'The winner stands alone' by Paulo Coelho today & I happened to come across this excerpt. I realised that the same thing happens with us humans every single day. We don't even have the excuse of different languages, most of the time, it's just our perspectives that differ so much. We fail to understand the point of view of anyone other than ourselves. Even if we are shown the other side for a while by a well-meaning friend or acquaintance, we conform to our originality sooner or later.

No matter how happy or content we may be with someone or something, we get back to our comfort zones as soon as circumstances permit. We cherish the memories. We think that all that happiness was an unattainable dream. Sometimes we pine for those lost times and opportunities too but we eventually move on. We get back to our bland, mundane lifestyles because that's what we are, that's who we have always been. In the process we lose our real chance at a blissful, different life.

All we had to do was to grow some wings. Believe in the vision of another. Give up the safety of our self – imposed confines, our perspectives, for once and take that leap into the unknown that could have landed us some place idyllic.

Alas! Our human stubbornness has been the doom of many a friendships & relationships. It has been the downfall of many a promising careers & success stories.

Two men looked through the same bars

One saw the mud , the other saw the stars.

True, we are each allowed to have and nurture our own sets of beliefs, our deductions, our logic. There is no harm in seeing things differently. But, differences in opinions are healthy only till they help us grow and evolve. When they start to deter our lives irrevocably, we need to sit up and take notice. We need to shun our prides, apologise and reclaim that little bit of heaven that we had found by some miracle.

Thankfully, there is a parallel reality for all of us. We just have to go through the looking glass and discover our own personal Magic ✨

Just a thought!

Caged

December 13, 2017

A cold winter morning.. The Sun peeking through the mist, trying to bring some warmth to the wet & moist earth along with my jittering limbs & the deepest cockles of my heart. I sit in my balcony, soaking up the pink sunlight, with a hot cuppa tea. This has become a steady course to counter cold mornings for me. The isolation imposed by silence, of being surrounded by people yet remaining just with my thoughts, listening to nothing but the white noise of my indefatigable & unrelenting mind and observing the world go by, have become therapeutic. I have the guilty pleasure of snooping into people's lives and imagining their stories just by noticing a tiny miniscule part of their days from my tenth floor balcony.

What remarkable lessons can be taken from seemingly ordinary existences!

I saw a child, barely five or six, rush to the terrace of his house, directly beneath my balcony, hence the movement caught my eye. He seemed to be carrying something. On closer inspection I saw a couple of rabbits, white & fluffy, snuggled up in his arms. He deposited his cuddly load in a deserted corner of the cold, bare terrace where the two lagomorphs, confused & scared by the intense attention, quickly found warmth in each other. The child stood up and for a while observed the inactive rabbits seeking warmth in each other.

He mustn't have liked the fact that he, the one who owned them, was being ignored. He tried to raise them from their cold & fear- induced torpor by stomping his feet hard on the floor, the sound made the pets snuggle even closer to each other.

The child tried again, this time with huge green leaves, to lure them to activity. And finally, when he couldn't get any movement out of them, he lifted one and placed it away from its mate. Finding himself alone, the rabbit responded to the child's stomping by running helter-skelter, this was not only fun for the child but also must have pleased him to see, something he was so fascinated by, respond to him. He began chasing the poor pet from one corner of the terrace to another. After about ten minutes, he got bored of this and chased the other rabbit around. Then, he called on his family members, his grandfather & father, to come have a look at his possessions, the pets. There must have been a child- like innocence and eagerness in this show of ownership. I saw him trying to force feed the animals, scaring them with all his foot stomping and repeatedly pulling & pinching them to show his tenderness and love. As his attention wavered, the rabbits, yet again, found a quiet corner to escape this ordeal. But the child wasn't done with them. Weren't they his pets? Wasn't it their duty to acknowledge and reciprocate his love?

He chased them, played with them, cuddled them, fed them, showed them off to others and yet could not get a puppy like tail-wagging appreciation of his attention and love so he CAGED them.

I sat there thinking. We don't change much as grown ups. Human love is possessive, protective and limiting, sometimes resembling a cage. We don't let go of the objects of our affection easily. We don't set them free & let them come back to us, of their own accord, instead, in order not to lose them, we chain and cage them to keep them safe and with us all the time. Our latent sense of protection and ownership smother the very people we love. Be it as parents, friends, spouses, or well- wishers, we always look out for the ones we love and there is nothing wrong in it. But too much of everything is bad. While 'looking out for' is a welcome emotion, setting boundaries and limiting someone's range out of love, reeks of negativity.

Not everyone is the same. Every species put on this planet understands love and God has given each a different way to express that love. While puppies and dogs have a special way of making us feel loved, adored and wanted, not all of the others can express it in the same way. Same applies to humans too. All of us love but our expression and needs are different. We have been endowed with something that other species don't have. It is the combination of speech and perception. Why can't we, then, use it to our benefit and make our relationships happier and more content?

After all, however gilded, a cage is a CAGE..

A Happy New Year

December 31, 2017

There are chants and wishes for a Happy New year today wherever we go..

There are celebrations galore..

There are hopes, dreams, aspirations & resolutions even for those who don't or won't party the night out to ring in the New Year..

And why not!! Do these changing dates on the calendar not fill us with hopes for a happier, healthier, brighter & better tomorrow? They do.. It's hope that make the world go round.

Amidst all this hullabaloo, let's not forget the less fortunate ones.

A compassionate friend of mine always says- "नानक दुखिया सब संसार" We think that our pain and our troubles are all that there is to this world.. But it isn't so...... The world is full of all kinds of suffering and misery.

Let's not overlook the ones whose life is a graver struggle in the absence of resources that we take for granted. Let's clear some space in our hearts and minds for those whose suffering never relents. Let's wish for a better tomorrow for them too. Let's be grateful for whatever little or plenty that the Almighty has bestowed on us. Let's resolve not to complain about our circumstances when there are others who would gladly swap lives with us. Let's try and look beyond ourselves and do something worthwhile this year for the ones who really need it...

Let us make this year count for us & for others..

I wish you and your family a very HAPPY NEW YEAR..

May this year see you through your trials, may it grant you courage to face adversities & overcome them, may there be triumphs and reasons to rejoice. Have a good one..

Reflections

February 16, 2018

Years back when I had just joined the teaching profession and was brimming with fresh ideas and ideals, I remember feeling indignant when a cousin of mine spoke to me about the caste card he would play to, in the upcoming elections. My cousin had some years on me and had pretty clear ideas how democracy worked at the grassroot level. I was shocked and indignant because his ideas did not match the ones given in the text book.

Some years on, when I had gained some worldly experience and knew of rage, oppression and fate dealing a lame card, I was still shocked when an extremely mild- mannered colleague of mine belonging to a marginal community, spoke harshly with an almost wolfish snarl what he thought of being secular.

His venomous hate for an entire community, though coming from personal experience, did not feel justified to me.

Quite recently, the brouhaha about the release of a movie on a long dead queen also felt unnecessary and roguish to me.

But isn't this where we make mistakes? What may be clear as crystal to me, may not even ring a bell with someone else. It's the perceptions that we form that make us the people we are.

And even if it has taken me years to get this simple fact straight, I now realise that respecting other people's way of looking at things makes life uncomplicated and hassle free. We cannot expect even our closest ones to feel exactly as we do on issues, both ideological and otherwise.

The more we read or expose ourselves to unfamiliar notions in any form, through any medium, the more we grow as a person.

While going through Adolf Hitler's autobiography Mein Kampf, I got to know why he hated the Jews so much. I may not agree with his beliefs, ideas & deductions but he wasn't wrong in his own eyes. His perception gave way to the Holocaust, the biggest genocide the world has ever experienced, and yet he was convinced that he was right all along.

Our beliefs are rooted in our own experiences. However bad a person may seem to the multitude, he is worth praising if he sticks to his beliefs. The ideas and notions of some may be repugnant to us or many others but they are there because they stand on the firm ground of experiences of that individual. That doesn't make it wrong. They may not be justified but are true for them.

What I don't get is being so impressionable that you can be swayed from what you truly believe, by dint of great oratory, fine language or the personality of a person.

Some of us have it easy. We haven't had bitter experiences to shape up our thinking but for that very purpose we have been endowed with the faculty of brains, cognition, comprehension, logic, deductions and free will.. If only, we could use them instead of being blind followers to anyone that can wield and plant a thought in our minds, the world would be a more peaceful place and our relationships more transparent.

Conundrum

February 24, 2018

If we try and hold on to everything at the same time, we lose everything in the process..

How many times have we read and heard it spoken, yet it hurts when it actually goes down.. There is no perfect world out there. Every moment in our lives comes with choices. Sometimes they are simple and easy to make and give us a freedom to go with what suits us best but there are times when we don't want to take the fork. We want the paths to merge so that we can have it all.

Every writer, worth his or her salt, has a Muse. Whether they know it or not, something or someone always acts like an inspiration or a cornerstone of their writings. They lay the foundations of their pieces around it and weave their magical yarn.

Our words flow when our Muse is somewhere in our minds.

To me, writer's block comes when I lose that vision or thought on whose foundation my words stand. It's true that I wrote earlier too but my writings started making sense to me with that presence in my mind. I realized quite late where the word flow came from. There was an extremely dry spell when I couldn't put my thoughts into any coherent sequence and I quit trying to write for those few months because even if I did try, it came out as a forced effort. Not honest, not sincere!

What that sabbatical from writing did, was another blessing. I found my Voice in the mean time! I found that writing was not the only thing that could be cathartic if you had a willing ear to hear you voice your opinions.

But life happens when you start settling down to change. When you start to get comfortable in the little haven that you have created, BAM! life hits you with a test. And it is cruel at times. It gives you the choice of Either Or.. It's more of a conundrum than a choice, actually. Either Or exists only when both the choices are hard to give up on. That's the whole idea behind it.

By some turn of fate, if I get back my Words, why should I be posed with the threat of losing my Voice?

Why can't both stay?

In a perfect world, they would!

👑The Indomitable Spirit👑

April 1, 2018

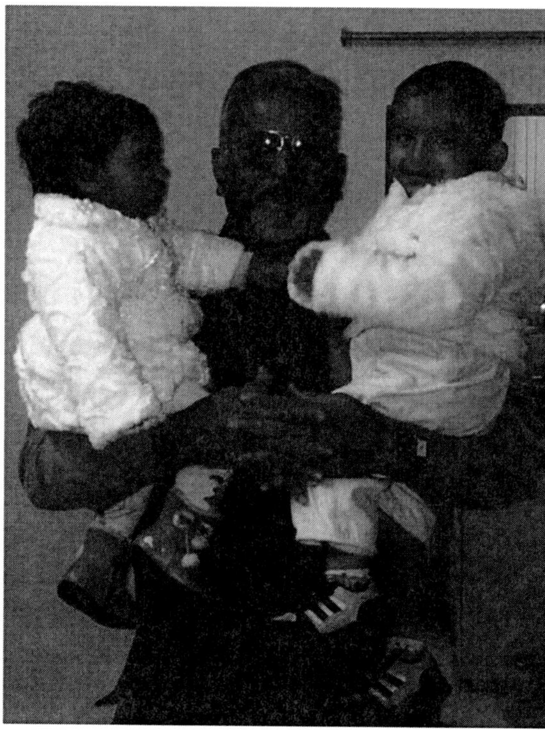

"Look, look, Guttu! Look at the color of her hair", Mishti, my six year old niece couldn't hold back her excitement when she saw an old lady with hair as white as cotton wool, nearly the same texture too. I explained to her how a human body ages and loses its vigour with time. She went into deep contemplation and didn't bring up the topic again until the next morning when we were riding towards her school astride our new activa. We happened to chance upon a fallen tree spread across the whole road. We had to careen awkwardly to make our way past it. She was curious as to what had happened to it. I again told her that it had aged and lost its strength and thus fallen down – dead. She was quick with her repartee, "Aged- just like the old woman we saw yesterday." I was overwhelmed with tenderness at her innocence and struggled to grapple with the fact as to how the notion of aging would be such an alien and enormous concept for a six year old.

At 38, I myself don't get the process completely. I do understand the weathered bodies, the sluggish gait, the dimming eye sight, the hardness of hearing, the memory loss, the confusion, the irritability & the failing health. What surprises me daily is the unbent, unyielding spirit residing in those broken weathered bodies, the strength of their spine in face of adversity, the far sightedness, the willingness to hear the opinion of their children, the things that they remember from a life well- lived, the patience and the untiring care they have for the family.

It is as if they refuse to wilt away like dying flowers. The indomitable human spirit puts them far higher on the totem pole than any other living thing.

True, there are moments of despair and helplessness in the face of circumstances, events or even physical disability but I see people rise above them by dint of sheer courage and lifeskills that they have mastered over the long years of their existence. Ailing parents can be as stubborn and uncompromising as children but they have the virtue of experience and forgiveness that gives them an extra edge.

It is obvious that a long lifetime means a lot of experiences- some good, some bad. Some memories are worth cherishing and there are others that turn into grudges and regrets. The idleness and inactivity of old age brings all of that, forth. It's not just the body that withers, the mind also crumbles and some of us tend to become grumpy with age.

I am amazed when I look at my septuagenarian father. He has had a tough life. He faced the society headlong while in his youth, took unconventional decisions, looked after the entire extended family, made something of himself with little or no help from people around. He became who he is, on his own steam. A lesser man would have given up in face of all that he went through. But he stood tall and strong and proud all his life. There are times now when he loses faith, thinks of himself as a toothless tiger but he always, always fights back. He gets up, dusts himself off and does what he does best- Dominate.. Age might have slowed his reflexes a bit but his mind stays razor sharp and his eyes miss nothing. After all these years, he still has his exclusive outlook on everything. He is opinionated, strong, honest and an idealist to the core. He calls a spade a spade and doesn't like to mince his words with nary a bother what the world would think of him. He overthinks. His belief in family and the concept of kith and kin is rock solid, despite the many blows & setbacks. At 72, he is still the anchor that holds our craft together.

For every child his/her father is a source of constant support & inspiration. For me, despite our occasional differences, he remains My Hero, who has surmounted innumerable odds and survived.

And what a life it has been!!!!

Someday Mishti will also know what aging with style and on one's own terms means, thanks to her NANA..

It's just like driving!

May 29, 2018

What happens when we first learn to drive a car or ride a bike? After the initial apprehensions, a sort of over confidence sets in and combined with the zest of youth, we tend to forgo speed limits, we test our boundaries, we take chances, we know that we would be able to control the vehicle even at that insane speed. We feel a special kind of independence at being able to do things on our own, a self reliance, if you may.

Once the novelty wears off, it becomes routine. Driving or riding may still be synonymous with liberty but the thrill is gone. Gone is the urge to take unnecessary risk. It merely becomes a means of getting things done. At this stage we are more aware of the potholes, the traffic and the wisdom of slowing down and letting others pass. We are surer and more confident of our skills. We learn how to manoeuvre our ride around tight corners, we become adept at getting by without applying abrupt brakes..

Yes, life is a lot like driving.. Infact it is just like driving!

Plan with a Capital 'S'

May 29, 2018

Where do you plan to go this vacation? How are you bringing in the new year/ your birthday / your anniversary? What do you plan to do in future? Are these the right courses for what you have in mind for your life? Why are you going out with this person, do you see a future with him or her? Have you been saving for a rainy day? Have you ensured that your children won't want for anything in their lives? Have you made sure that they have a sound financial backing as long as they live?

Sound familiar? The mental checklist!!! The grocery list for life. We have all been taught not to disregard it. We have all been brought up to think and over think like that. We think and think and then think some more. We plan, we propose, we toil, we execute and in the end we have successful lives with enough financial security to last us a lifetime and some of us even go beyond that and take care of our next generation too.

We marry, have a family. Sometimes we fall in love too and then again we analyse whether that (person /relationship) would work in our lives or not. We hold on to it if it fits with our master plan and let go if it doesn't.

All of it is highly rational and responsible behaviour. We have to keep up the family name, its legacy which is the biggest thing we pass on to our children. It cannot be tainted by impulsive acts or decisions, can it be?

But just for a moment think, what if we could lead our lives without planning ahead? What if, we concentrated more on OUR lives alone not burdened by the family name, or what people would say or what will happen if plan A fails!! We have been brought up to think of all possible scenarios. We have a master plan A, if that fails we fall back on Plan B, God forbid if that fails we either have a workable Plan C or we give in to despair. Assign it to fate. Lose hope. Sometimes we muster courage to pick ourselves up and fight back. Isn't that what all great success stories, that we keep hearing for inspiration, are about?

What I am suggesting here is something completely different. Something, few have the courage and audacity to take up. I am referring to a Super Plan S, where S stands for SPONTANEITY. What would it be like to live life as it comes? Wouldn't it be more meaningful if it is led as God wanted us to lead it- without frills & attachments. It would be a great relief if we could start a relationship, a job, a move, an education without thinking— WHAT NEXT!!

Isn't it enough that we are living it up in the moment?

How many of the 'successful' people, we look upto, have lived their lives without compromises? It's a cliché choice – happiness or success. I am not posing that question here. It is perfectly alright to want to be successful in life. It is great to be ambitious but not the same rules apply to all people.

live the life you love

For me success might not mean money. For me happiness might not mean success. I may be happy in a relationship without a future. I may find contentment even in the absence of high living. I might be fulfilled without a soul mate or in some cases a life partner.

It is different for each person and it is alright for him or her to make those choices without pressure from family, relatives or well meaning friends. We are not going to take back anything from here. Not the money we earn, nor the good deeds we perform.

We are here to keep our Souls happy. We form attachments along the way- some we are born into, others we cultivate but our prime responsibility is to ourselves. We cannot pour from an empty cup. To be able to give happiness, we have to be happy inside. There is no perfect recipe for it which suits all palates. How we find it, nurture it, is upto each individual..

“Welcome To Wherever You Are”

June 2, 2018

It was just that sort of a day when you need to remind yourself of who you are and what your core is made of. Actually, it’s been a series of such days end on end.

Being a bibliophile, I try and find answers in the written word. For me, there is nothing that a google search can’t throw up- from books on recipes to countering depression, from what to watch in which mood to what to wear and where & how to travel, from ailments and their cures to the composition and impact of medicines, I find everything when I look for it and more often than not, I end up reading on everything that goes on in my mind. That’s how much words rule me.

So, it wasn't surprising when I noticed some discrepancies in my general behaviour and reactions, I immediately looked up the reason for the change and found out that there is something called 'working depression' & that I was quietly but steadily moving towards it. On delving into the problem further, I found out about (surprise, surprise!) a book- Pilgrimage of Desire by Alison Gresik.

Generally, I don't read self help books but this is something that all of us can benefit from. I am still on it and I feel better because I realise that we are not alone in this. All of us go through lean patches and we have got to believe that there is a way out of them. And once we are out of them, we shine brighter. We may not come out unscathed but they are just battle wounds, the scars that leave a memory and a lesson.

Years ago, a friend of mine introduced me to the marvel, that is, Jon Bon Jovi and one of his songs that is etched deep into my psyche is 'Welcome to wherever you are', the other being 'Walk like a man'. I may have spoken about the latter in one of my previous pieces but the former is the one that inspires me in my current mood.

I leave you with the lyrics and will try and attach a link to it too.

Happy listening!

Maybe we're all different, but we're still the same..

We all got the blood of Eden, running through our veins.

I know sometimes it's hard for you to see.

You are caught between just who you are and who you wanna be.

If you feel alone, and lost and need a friend

Remember every new beginning, is some beginning's end.

Welcome to wherever you are

This is your life, you made it this far.

Welcome, you gotta believe

That right here right now, you're exactly where you're supposed to be.

Welcome, to wherever you are..

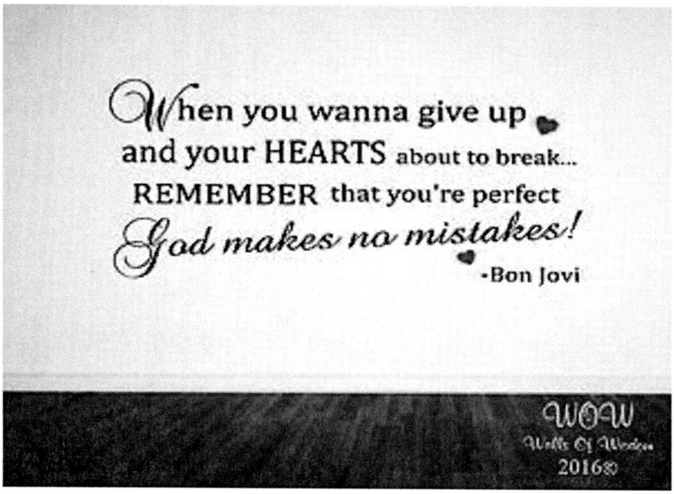

When everybody's in, and you're left out

And you feel you are drowning, in a shadow of a doubt.

Everyones a miracle in their own way

Just listen to yourself, not what other people say.

When it seems you're lost, alone and feeling down

Remember everybody's different

Just take a look around.

Welcome to wherever you are

This is your life, you made it this far

Welcome, you gotta believe

That right here right now, you're exactly where you're supposed to be.

Be who you want to, be who you are

Everyone is a hero, everyone is a star..

When you wanna give up, and your heart is about to break.

Remember that you're perfect, God makes no mistakes.

Welcome to wherever you are

This is your life, you made it this far

Welcome, you gotta believe

That right here right now, you're exactly where you're supposed to be

Welcome, to wherever you are.

Welcome to wherever you are

🙏Making Amends🙏

June 8, 2018

What is the gravest loss a person can incur? Someone frivolous would say- Money, someone with greater depth and realisation about how life runs would say – passing away or passing on of loved ones is a loss that can never be repaired. True that!

But while we are living, we learn to survive with or without people. Even if they pass on, we can find solace in the fact that they loved and cherished us as we do them.

In my very humble opinion, the greatest loss a person can lay oneself open to is the loss of respect, whether it is in the eyes of our loved ones or in our own judgement.

It isn't rocket science to understand that not all of us are destined for great things, not all of us would be remembered by a multitude, not all of us would earn the celebrity status, few amongst us will earn a handsome living but there runs a common thread between the greats and the ordinary ones, like us.

All of us have one Life and we need to prioritize it in such a way that we make the extraordinary come alive even in the mundane. We may not be a Ratan Tata, an Indra Nooyi, an Amitabh Bachchan, a Lata Mangeshkar, a Mark Zuckerberg or a Steve Jobs to inspire an entire generation but we are humans too and it is upto us to be exemplary atleast to our own children.

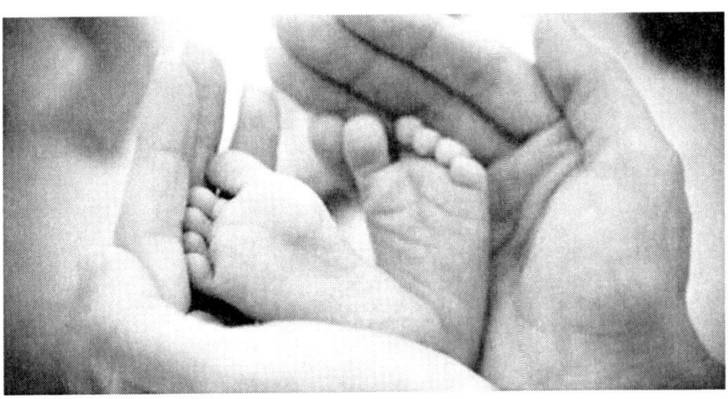

I have written time and again about how I look upto both my parents for everything in my life. The way they have led theirs, their experiences and conduct even in the face of adversity, their even temperaments, their integrity and honesty have far surpassed any flaws that are bound to seep into a human character. I am proud to be their daughter although sometimes theirs are huge shoes to fill in.

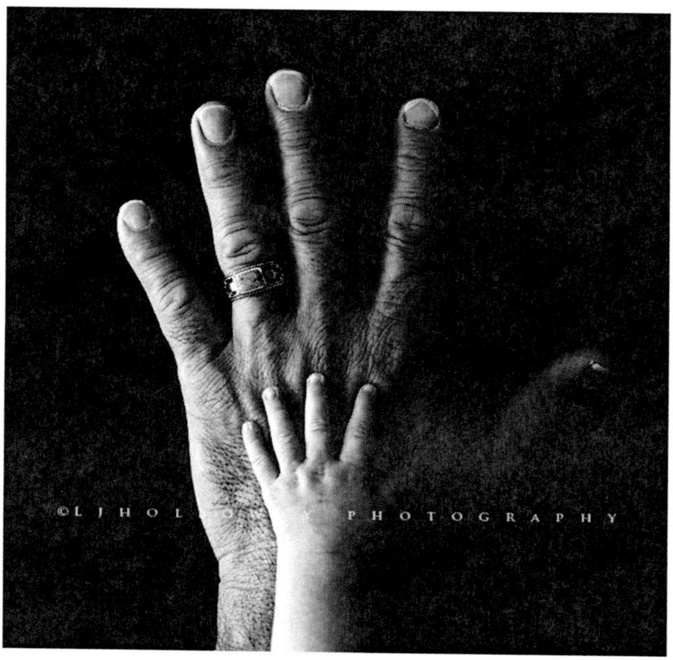

It's not always that, parenting goes right. I may not be the most appropriate person to talk about it but I have observed, at close quarters, children losing respect for their fathers or mothers. It used to baffle me because it was a completely alien concept for me. How could one hate one's parent? Way back in my school days, I had some classmates who rarely spoke about or to their mothers. Being an impressionable child myself, I had spoken to my mother about it and she had wisely advised me not to be judgemental or take sides, better still to mind my own business and not put my nose where it wasn't required.

With years and age came maturity and a kind of experienced comprehension of human nature. During my teaching years, I came across a couple of girls who hated their mothers. For one it was easily explained – she had a step mom and the girl had never warmed up to her but there was another who just couldn't tolerate her own natural mother. Try as I may, I couldn't understand that kind of hatred.

Some years on, I moved back to my hometown to be with my parents and thus nearer to my extended family too. True, it is trying, living with people of a generation that doesn't understand your reasons and don't approve of your way of doing things and true, there are disagreements too but at the end of the day, they are our parents and we learn from their experiences. Wherever necessary, we also tell them a better way of handling things. Hate never enters this equation. Not with the parents atleast. But that's me and my life. Not everyone has the same circumstances.

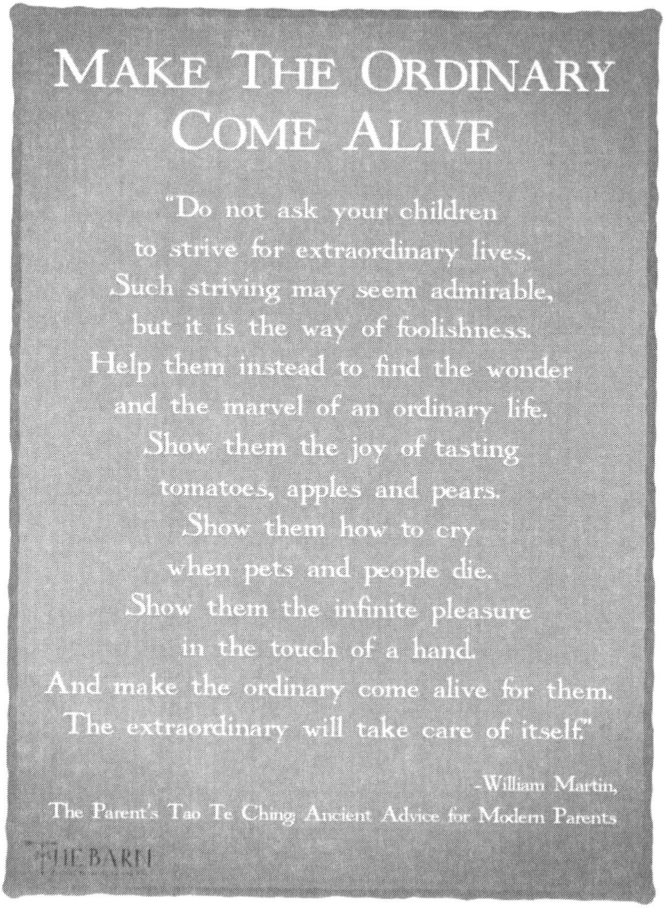

Today, more than anything, I understand the wisdom behind my mother's words when she had told me not to be too inquisitive about the lives of my friends and more specifically – never to judge. 'You don't know their truths. Not the same applies to everyone', was her constant reply to my curious wonderings.

I have seen grown men losing respect, losing face in front of their own kids. They can't handle the ever increasing pressures of modern day living and give in to vices like drinking to drown their sorrows, gambling to earn an easy buck, borrowing to pay back previous debts. It is a vicious circle. Instead of facing life headlong with grit and determination, they succumb to weaknesses of the body and soul which eats away at their family lives.

Far from being heroes or inspiration to their kids, they become embarrassments for their families. The impact on the children is life altering. They either become copies of their fathers, taking up those vices as their own or end up hating their parent and going against anything and everything they suggest. Either ways, lives get ruined.

This is the problem, but is there any use writing about the problem without suggesting a solution? My solution is simple and has to come from within.

Marriage is not just a social obligation that we have to perform when the time is right, instead it is a responsibility which should be taken only when one is ready for it. Becoming a parent makes one accountable. We don't have to lead extraordinary lives in order to earn the respect of our children, we just have to make our decisions on the basis of what will be right or wrong for our family as a whole.

Seemingly ordinary lives can also be remarkable if the children come out cultured, if they value their resources, are intellectually & morally sound and most importantly if they respect their elders, effortlessly.

We should give them reasons for that respect. Just because they are our offsprings is not enough cause for 'demanding' respect. How we conduct ourselves, goes a long way in shaping the lives and characters of our children. We cannot expect them to outshine us when all we are giving them is a lot of negative energy.

Having said that, we have one life too and at times we also can be reckless and experimental. We may enjoy our little indulgences but responsibility towards our children wins the round, hands down. We cannot drink ourselves to hell at the cost of our family just because we happen to enjoy our daily pint. We cannot smoke away to lala land without a thought about its impact on our family. We may take calculated risks to earn big time but cannot be reckless enough to go beyond our means and set up a debt for our children to repay. That's not how exemplary lives are lead.

Parenting with Passion

It's never too late to make amends. If our intentions are right and if our hearts are in the right place then we know what is the most important thing for a person- it's the love and respect of the ones closest to us. And make no mistake, we have to work hard to earn that. The first step is to acknowledge our mistakes and then try to mend our ways as best as possible. Even if we don't succeed in bringing in more money or stability to our lives atleast we can be content that we tried our best and that too with integrity.

Wouldn't it be endearing to be remembered as a good human being, once we are gone? Why just talk about being remembered once we are gone!! Wouldn't it warm the cockles of our hearts if people look up to us even in life? Wouldn't it be remarkable to leave a legacy of righteousness and morality for our kids to follow and pass on?

Start making amends today. We don't know what is in store for us tomorrow.

Learn to Listen

July 8, 2018

The incident, I am about to narrate, goes back to the year 2009 or 2010, I was teaching at a residential school then. We had an English department full of experienced and knowledgeable teachers, each more impressive than the next in terms of vigour, zest or plain perspective.

I remember the day like it was yesterday. Some of us were sitting in the staff room carrying on with our respective tasks when Ma'am Santosh Ahlawat entered. I was in awe of her personality. Tall and distinguished, she seemed to be at complete ease in her skin. Her smiling face and radiance gave the impression of a person who had things under control and one who was sure of herself in every way. Nothing seemed to bother her or ruffle her feathers. She had great ideas too. It may seem like my personal ode to her but the fact of the matter is that I didn't know her well enough and all the attributes, I have just mentioned about her, have only come to my mind now that I have sat down to write.

The only thing that I truly and vividly remember about her is what she told us that day and which has somehow stuck with me over the years. A simple thought but of great import. She had just come to the staffroom after taking an impromptu class with grade 9th. As it was an unscheduled period, she just gave them a random idea, wrote it on the green board and asked them to ponder over it. Her notion, though basic, was extremely profound. On the board she had written – LEARN TO LISTEN.

This tiny piece of sparkling wisdom has stayed with me since then. I keep telling the people or students I come in contact with, 'to listen' as much as they can. Over the years, I have benefitted a lot by cultivating this miniscule, seemingly random, bit of virtue.

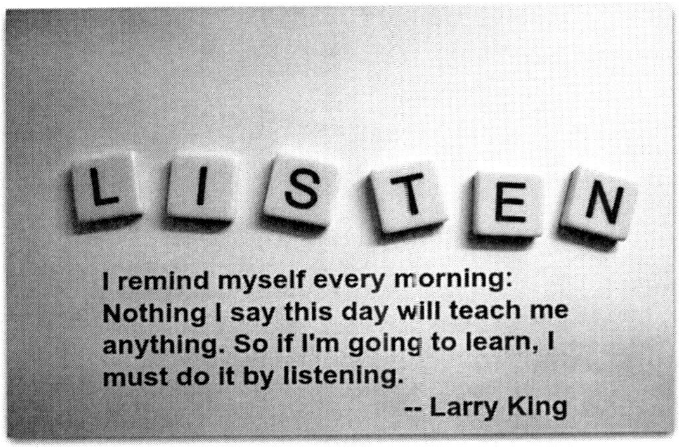

It's true that we learn new things only when we shut up & listen to new ideas and perspectives. People feel respected around us if, all we do, is listen to them make their point. We pick up new languages when we listen to natives speaking them. We earn the respect and admiration of our colleagues and subordinates when we let them make their case by giving them a chance to speak. For teachers and parents, earning the trust and devotion of their students or children is the greatest achievement, which is possible only when we listen to them. Not only these practical, day to day things, we also appreciate nature more when we sit quietly and observe its various bounties. We may have gathered and accumulated a lot of knowledge and experience but that doesn't make us all-knowing.

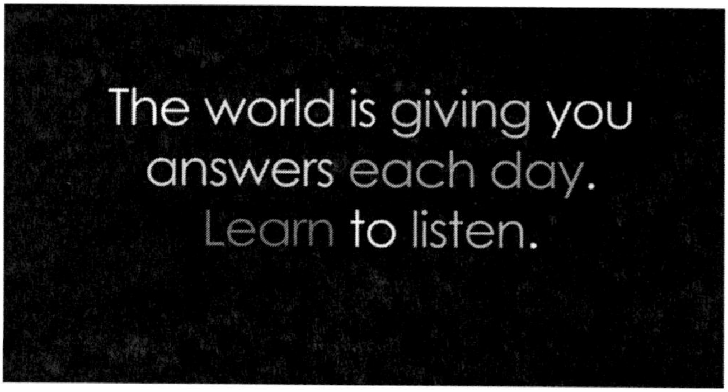

Each of us has a lot to learn about the blessing that this human birth is, about the people around us and how to treat them, about nature, God, life, our work, relationships, about things that are said but not meant or others that are meant but never said, about situations that we find ourselves in and the tight corners that we have to manoeuvre around, about events that are evident but not real or real but not apparent or discernable.

Our lives would seem inadequate or insufficient in terms of time or length if we decide to pay heed to whatever there is to learn. But if we have to grow, that is the only path to take. Books and success stories can only teach us as much.

We genuinely learn from our environment and that too only when we give it an opportunity to make an impact on us. The easiest and the most pragmatic course of action would be to Listen. Listening is not just hearing but paying attention to not only the words spoken but also to those meant. Listening is not a stimuli for answering or replying or hitting back, it is a stepping stone for comprehension, reformation and change.

Recently, I was reading Sapiens by Yuval Noah Harari and I read that the only thing that made Homo Sapiens different from other Humans and animals was the size of our brains. We are the wise ones. Ours is a chosen species. What we choose to do with this life is upto us! We can either stick to the comfortable and stay happy in our ignorance or else venture out of that safe zone, step into the unknown and find bliss that would add meaning to our mundane lives.

Wasn't it Anand (Rajesh Khanna) who said, "बाबू मोशाय, ज़िन्दगी बड़ी होनी चाहिए, लंबी नही" Life should be meaningful (big/large) not long (as in years without any real wisdom)

The one thing that we can all promise ouselves to do in our ordinary lives is to be open to learning and that would be possible only when we learn to listen.

Just a thought!

†Crosses we bear†

July 8, 2018

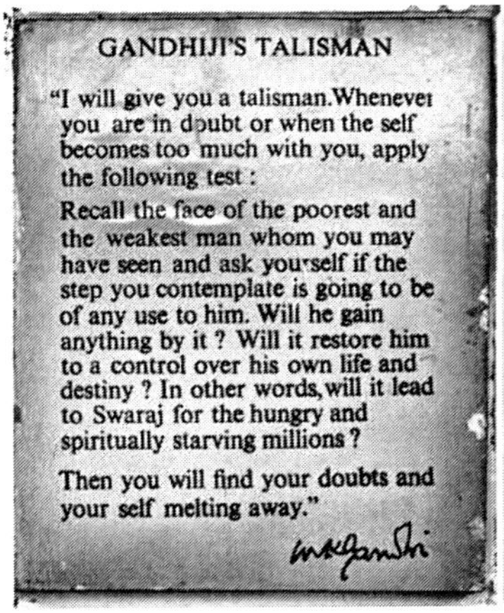

GANDHIJI'S TALISMAN

"I will give you a talisman.Whenever you are in doubt or when the self becomes too much with you, apply the following test :

Recall the face of the poorest and the weakest man whom you may have seen and ask yourself if the step you contemplate is going to be of any use to him. Will he gain anything by it ? Will it restore him to a control over his own life and destiny ? In other words,will it lead to Swaraj for the hungry and spiritually starving millions ?

Then you will find your doubts and your self melting away."

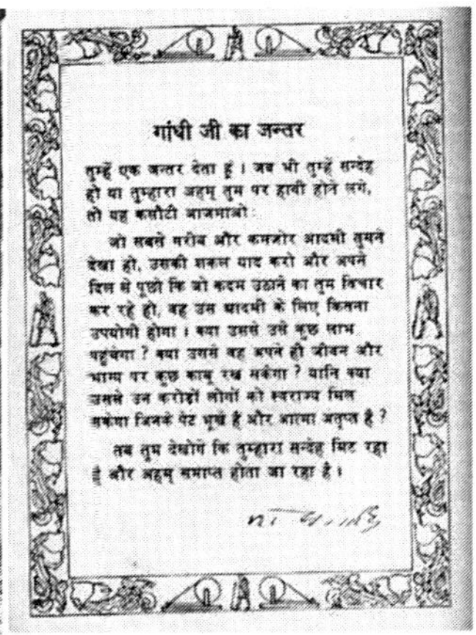

गांधी जी का जन्तर

तुम्हें एक जन्तर देता हूं। जब भी तुम्हें सन्देह हो या तुम्हारा अहम् तुम पर हावी होने लगे, तो यह कसौटी आजमाओ:

जो सबसे गरीब और कमजोर आदमी तुमने देखा हो, उसकी शकल याद करो और अपने दिल से पूछो कि जो कदम उठाने का तुम विचार कर रहे हो, वह उस आदमी के लिए कितना उपयोगी होगा। क्या उससे उसे कुछ लाभ पहुंचेगा? क्या उससे वह अपने ही जीवन और भाग्य पर कुछ काबू रख सकेगा? यानि क्या उससे उन करोड़ों लोगों को स्वराज्य मिल सकेगा जिनके पेट भूखे हैं और आत्मा अतृप्त है?

तब तुम देखोगे कि तुम्हारा सन्देह मिट रहा है और अहम् समाप्त होता जा रहा है।

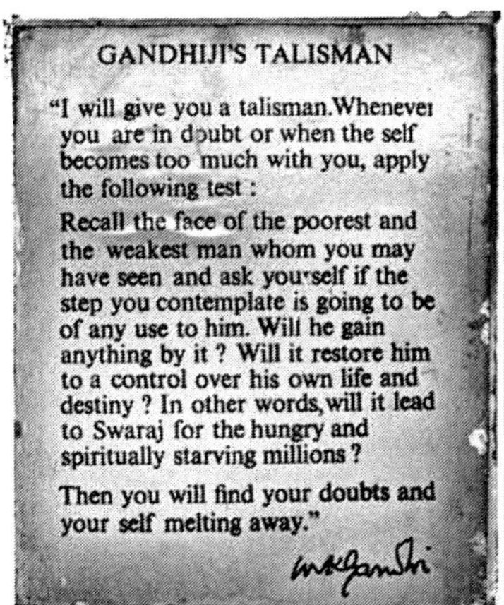

GANDHIJI'S TALISMAN

"I will give you a talisman.Whenever you are in doubt or when the self becomes too much with you, apply the following test :

Recall the face of the poorest and the weakest man whom you may have seen and ask yourself if the step you contemplate is going to be of any use to him. Will he gain anything by it ? Will it restore him to a control over his own life and destiny ? In other words,will it lead to Swaraj for the hungry and spiritually starving millions ?

Then you will find your doubts and your self melting away."

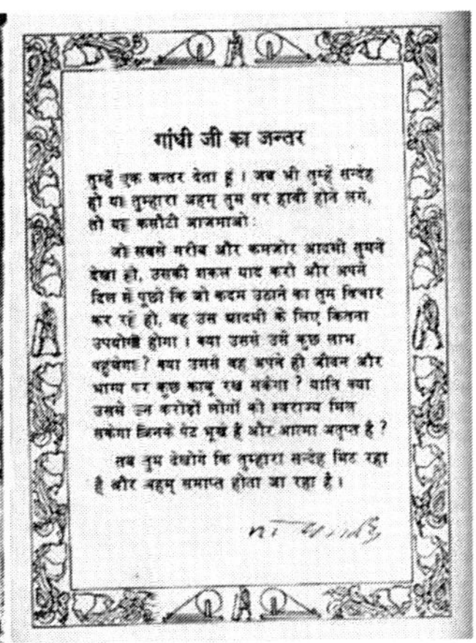

गांधी जी का जन्तर

तुम्हें एक जन्तर देता हूं। जब भी तुम्हें सन्देह हो या तुम्हारा अहम् तुम पर हावी होने लगे, तो यह कसौटी आजमाओ:

जो सबसे गरीब और कमजोर आदमी तुमने देखा हो, उसकी शकल याद करो और अपने दिल से पूछो कि जो कदम उठाने का तुम विचार कर रहे हो, वह उस आदमी के लिए कितना उपयोगी होगा। क्या उससे उसे कुछ लाभ पहुंचेगा? क्या उससे वह अपने ही जीवन और भाग्य पर कुछ काबू रख सकेगा? यानि क्या उससे उन करोड़ों लोगों को स्वराज्य मिल सकेगा जिनके पेट भूखे हैं और आत्मा अतृप्त है?

तब तुम देखोगे कि तुम्हारा सन्देह मिट रहा है और अहम् समाप्त होता जा रहा है।

Many of you might remember the old NCERT textbooks which had one page right at the beginning sharing the Talisman propounded by Mahatma Gandhi.

At the time, I didn't completely get the meaning of his words which are now crystal clear.

What Gandhiji meant when he gave us that mantra was – there are always people more unfortunate than us and that every step, every action undertaken by us should be carried out keeping in mind the welfare of those less fortunate ones.

My piece here lays down no such lofty ideals. I just want to underline the fact that each of us thinks that the troubles and trials of our lives are unique and beyond endurance. But in essence, life isn't easy for any of us. We just have to make the best of what is given to us.

There are people who are enduring terminal illnesses, there are some who have been turned out of their own homes by their own flesh and blood, others still lead lives of penury and want, there are many who are either too fat or too thin, some suffer physical handicaps others mental ailments, there are yet others who have no talent or scope for education and few who are low on luck despite the degrees, some are financially well off but have no mental peace others can't make two ends meet. For some there are marital troubles for others relationships are difficult. Some are in agony because they are childless some worry because they have too many mouths to feed. There are some for whom their sexuality or gender is a cross, they are born that way, others still whose choices society doesn't accept.

In nutshell, as long as we have human lives, we have desires. These desires are the root cause of pain. The unending want for more create a gloom and unhappiness that is beyond our control. We suffer because we always want something that has not been served to us. We suffer because we constantly compare our lives with others. For us grass is always greener on the other side of the fence. We don't acknowledge the fact that the grass is greener where it is watered.

We cry and make a hullabaloo about the suffering we have to sustain. We pray to our Gods to alleviate our burdens. We cut corners, we try and cheat fate and hoodwink our destiny. All in vain.

We have been given one life. True, it has some challenges. We each have our crosses to bear and carry but if we do so with a song in our heart and a smile on our lips, won't it be more convenient and bearable?

Nobody's life is a bed of roses. We all have crosses to bear and we all just do our best.

Yoko Ono

In any case we have to live through the entire span of life given to us. Why not face it headlong without complaining and cribbing about it.. Why make it tougher than it already is? We can strive to improve our lot in life, that's our right and prerogative but there really isn't any use lamenting the things we lack or the burdens we have to carry. We won't die before it is our time so why not live it up despite the tests assigned to us.

Think about it!

Losing Inhibitions

July 29, 2018

I make it a point not to write anything while I am into a book and to be honest, I can't think of anything worth writing other than the subject of the book I am on, while it lasts. But we come across so many things in life that need addressing and more often than not, the solution to those are rarely found in books.

I take a class of English language communication with a senior group and recently one of the group members came upto me and told me that he didn't think the class was working for him. It wasn't as if the subject matter or delivery was difficult to get. It was just that he felt a lot of hesitation in front of his female counterparts. He was specific that his fear of or inability to interact with people of the opposite sex went beyond the classroom even to the social sphere. He conceded that to stay abreast with the world today, he needed to lose this shackle. I had noticed such fearful tendencies in other group members too.

ILLUSTRATION BY MARCI SUELA | SPARTAN DAILY

I applaud him for having the courage to accept and discuss the leash that bound him, with me. I got thinking and realised that without actually registering, we make habits of certain things. Most of our mannerism and the way we carry ourselves in our lives, come from the things which may not be taught verbally at home but are observed and ingrained passively.

I find this hesitation and inhibition a regular feature of life in small town India. Rarely, have I come across families or parents who have managed to give a broad minded upbringing to their kids. The fear of speaking or performing in front of a gathering or group of people from the opposite sex is more common in adults than in children.

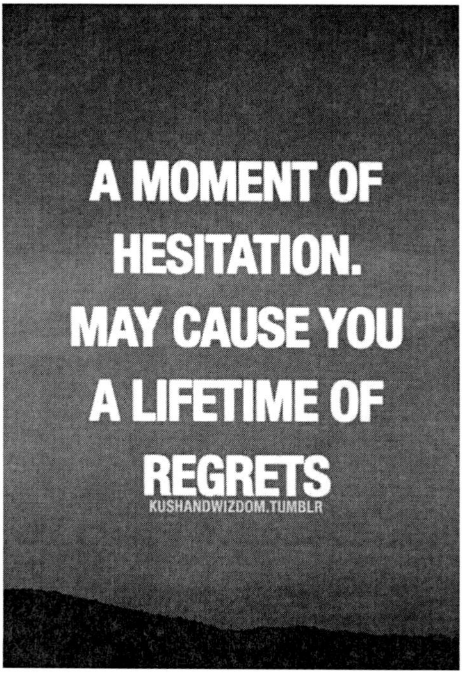

As we grow older we get more and more negatively conditioned at home & in the society. The gender difference, that cannot be denied by anyone in our small city lives, comes in the way of living freely. Even Co-educational institutions try and keep the two sexes in separate columns. In classrooms, we have separate rows and columns for girls and boys, in sports there are separate teams, for cultural functions, girls prepare a separate piece and the boys stay in their own spheres. Out of school, parents don't allow friends from the other sex to mix up with us. Together, the schools and parents, condition a child so negatively that after an age even brother-sisters and cousins feel awkward around each other.

Do we think that keeping them separate like this would solve all the gender related issues and crimes that we come across in newspapers daily? In my humble opinion, if we stop them from doing anything, they would definitely want to go down that road. And mind you, when they do, it will all be hidden from parental scrutiny.

Isn't it better parenting if we move with the times and acknowledge that on reaching teens our children require knowledge and guidance on this issue? Won't it be preferable if our kids have the confidence that whatever it is they feel about anyone, they can share at home?

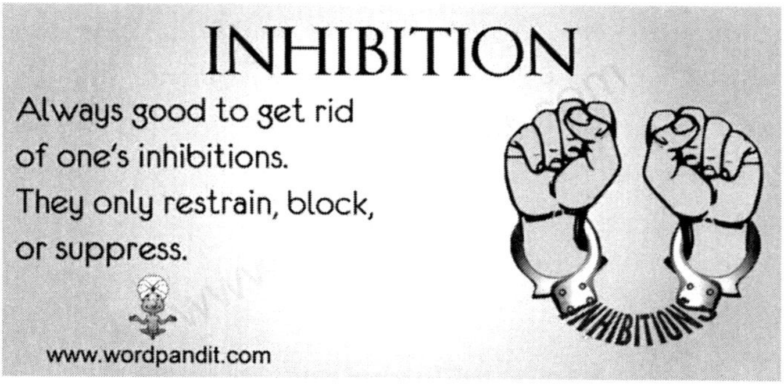

We were that age, not so long back and we cannot hide from the fact that human body and mind undergo a lot of change in our teens. Raging hormones are not an issue to be pushed under the rug and the solution is not to get our kids married young. We conform to the social traditions and maintain a steady gap between us and the kids in their growing up years. That ensures a fear and respect that fathers think they deserve but isn't love between parents and the kids more important? Does maintaining distance from our kid, when he or she is growing up, make us more respectable in the society or is it just an exercise for boosting the self? To keep up that facade of respect and fear intact, we arrange marriages for our children without even asking them whether they wish to get married at that age or whether they have someone they would like us to meet as a perspective life partner. Limited by inhibitions, most children do as they are told. No wonder then, that we have such soul less, unhappy marriages wherever we look. Life becomes a compromise for both partners concerned.

Our children fear us and in the absence of any kind of guidance from us on matters related to sex, they turn to the next best option- their classmates or seniors, who have had a similar upbringing. But even that is passé now. Like everything else, the children find answers on the internet. Do you think that information, thus gleaned, is healthy for a balanced mental growth of a child?

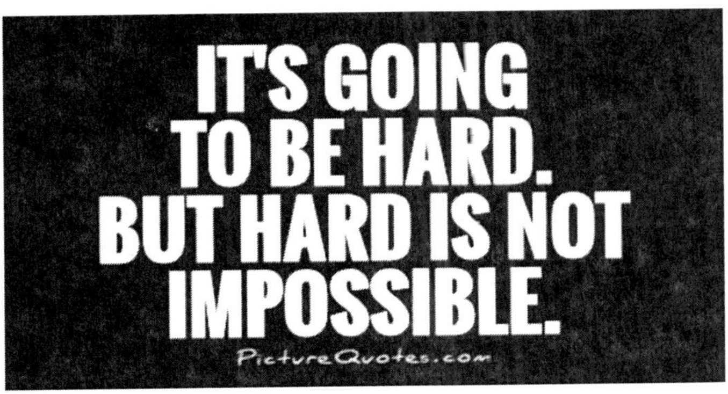

Such trends don't bode well for us as a society. I agree, things are changing but we still need to earn that confidence of our children if we want them to confide in us. We should be grown up enough to give them choices. After a point, a person can be a judge of what is right or wrong for him/her. Believe me, the values that we so painstakingly inculcate and grind into our children day in and day out, will stay with them when the time comes. We should have faith in their decisions and our efforts invested in them. If we don't stand by them, when they make life – altering choices, who will? Unless we give up this medieval thought process that programs us to control every aspect of our child's life, we will not be able to bring up confident, decisive, content, happy individuals that our children should be.

Let them out. Don't curtail their innocent freedoms. Let them make friends on the basis of who they gel with instead of on narrow considerations of gender & caste. Let them choose- their lives, their friends, their jobs, their partners & their happiness.

🤔The Query🤔

August 6, 2018

Years ago, as a child, I remember being herded into a Saint's presence along with my mother, siblings and scores of strangers vying for the hallowed vision. I recall my confusion at people coming up with questions for the enlightened one and he seemed to be at ease answering them. My mother didn't put up a question and we left, having benefitted from the 'darshan' alone.

Some years on, when influenced by my immediate circle of friends, I was fascinated with astrology and palmistry, (I am reminded of a phase when I bought and religiously read books on the two disciplines), I went to a celebrated astrologist of my city, someone who had the reputation of always 'see'ing through to a person's future. After an initial analysis of my lines and birth chart, he prompted me to ask questions. I was in a fix. What should one ask? One who believes in karma and one who takes all decisions of life in a precise, calculative, no-nonsense manner, how should such a person ask someone for speculative guidance to her own life?

A lot of water has flown under the bridge since then. Life, responsibilities, challenges have matured me from that moony eyed romantic to a pragmatic skeptic. I have read voraciously all these years and tried looking for answers to life in the written word.

It is true that the question of what lies in the future troubles us at times but it can be fathomed through our educated guesses. What we sow, so shall we reap!

There is a query, though, which I find unsatisfactorily attended to in most books I have read or by people I have spoken to.

Every human being has to play various roles in this life. We are sons, daughters, sisters, brothers, friends, lovers, husbands, wives, parents, grandparents, professionals, homemakers, neighbours, relatives, citizens; all folded into one multidimensional personality. What I fail to come to terms with is- Which identity to accept? Most of our multiple roles have a tendency of coming into conflict with each other, time and again. We find it difficult to keep all our ducks in a row. We are rarely able to provide a semblance of order to every aspect of our life. A little bit of management is all right for everyone and it doesn't induce a lot of heartache to relinquish control over or give up on certain unimportant duties, chores or even relationships. But this choice is nearly impossible to make when two or more equally significant parts of our life are pit against each other. It becomes herculean to accomplish everything at once. If we try to put one decision in effect, we sometimes lose another. How do we strike this balance?

I have read that one should learn to put oneself first, that one cannot pour from an empty cup, that one's happiness attracts all the positive energy and gets things done, that when we are happy we can make others smile too. But these lessons look good in print, I have never been able to really put them into practice.

So, if I have to raise just one query of a 'holy see', or a 'guru' or any life coach, I would want to know how to perceive myself, so that at least the people and situations important to me in life, won't suffer? I would ask them when to give in and how much of me to surrender?

On Healing

October 17, 2018

Do you believe in Karma? As Indians I know, most of us do. 'What goes round comes round,' is the theory our lives revolve around.

It has been a year full of upheavals- physical, emotional, financial and any other 'al' that's possible. So what begot them? Is it just the move to a new space or the lack of religious peity? Is it the negative energy of the new place or the evil eye cast on us by seemingly well meaning friends and acquaintances?

Why blame someone or something for one's ill-fortune? I believe we reap what we sow. No one is bad in his or her own perception and decent people don't go about planning to harm others with their words, actions or existences but try as we might we cannot please everyone and even without meaning to, we end up bringing grief to others. And grief thus brought, counts as a debit on one's account. It is all checks and balances from there on.

We do everything possible to cast off the negativity. We mostly give in to the tried and tested method– Religion. Sadly, we have been brought up to fear God more than we respect and love Him. So we fall into the trap of the self- appointed faith healers, the one's who claim a divine connect and we perform all sorts of weird things that normally and rationally we wouldn't. We hear stories of how such practices brought about a change in other people's lives. And we are tempted to try each one of them. Getting a havan or a special pooja done on an auspicious day is just the beginning. There is weirder stuff we all are acquainted with. Feeding the strays on a particular day of the week, feeding them specific stuff, eating something or abstaining from somethings come next. Then enters woodoo, black magic, tantras and mantras. We do everything and we believe in everything when the chips are down. Even my writing against them would be considered blasphemous by my equally rational family who have been bowed down in having faith in such stuff.

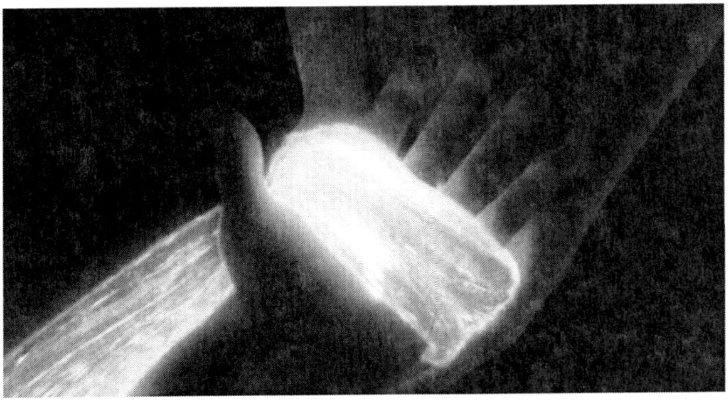

If not this what is the solution then? I believe the solution lies within us. One has to go through life without judgements, sans the feeling that ill things happen to me always. We have to have faith in God and his sense of justice. He wouldn't give us a burden too heavy for us to carry. Yes, there may be hardships but just like good times don't last, bad ones don't either. Life is a mix of both. Our problem is that we don't rejoice in the good times, they are taken as a matter of right while we whine away during the painful periods. Pain is inevitable. Whether it is loss of health, wealth, mental peace, a loved one- everything brings us pain. As humans, we just need to learn to accept what is given to us. We will start HEALING, the moment we realise that it is just life with its ebbs and flows, its triumphs and sorrows. No one else is responsible for what we face in life. It is just our actions that beget reactions. No amount of guilt can make life easy but acceptance can. If we recognise where we went wrong, we need to accept it without guilt, rectify it if we can, take a lesson and move on. There is no use crying over spilt milk. We can't undo our actions, however digital we get. We can just correct them and learn from what transpired. We are humans and are bound to falter in life but that shouldn't stop us from growing and experimenting and living.

As for religion, I have always felt that spirituality is much more important than being overtly religious. Then again, to each his or her own. Believing in God is important but a Punishing God is just the figment of our imaginations and a very popular one at that, specially in our society. God doesn't work that way.

Healing has to start from US and our unwavering faith in the goodness of life and judiciousness of the Almighty.

Hugs can heal. Listening can heal. Being there for someone can heal. Music can heal. Words and actions can heal. A kind heart can heal. It is the super power of us humans. We can Heal.

I don't know why but I am reminded of Rudyard Kipling's masterpiece of a poem- 'If', so I would leave you with that.

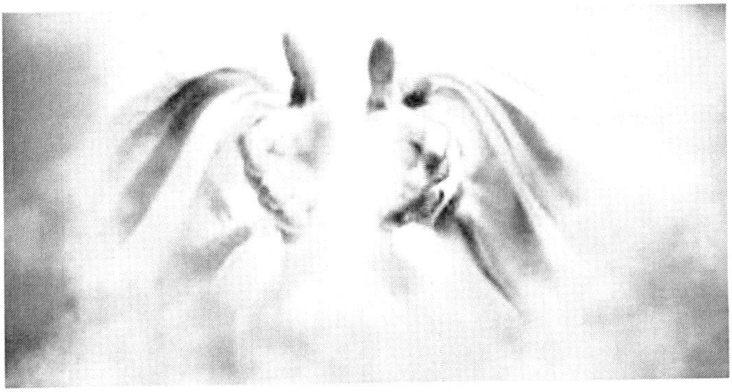

If you can keep your head when all about you
Are losing theirs and blaming it on you,
If you can trust yourself when all men doubt you,
But make allowance for their doubting too;
If you can wait and not be tired by waiting,
Or being lied about, don't deal in lies,
Or being hated, don't give way to hating,
And yet don't look too good, nor talk too wise:
If you can dream—and not make dreams your master;
If you can think—and not make thoughts your aim;
If you can meet with Triumph and Disaster
And treat those two impostors just the same;
If you can bear to hear the truth you've spoken
Twisted by knaves to make a trap for fools,
Or watch the things you gave your life to, broken,
And stoop and build 'em up with worn-out tools:

If you can make one heap of all your winnings
And risk it on one turn of pitch-and-toss,
And lose, and start again at your beginnings
And never breathe a word about your loss;
If you can force your heart and nerve and sinew
To serve your turn long after they are gone,
And so hold on when there is nothing in you
Except the Will which says to them: 'Hold on!'
If you can talk with crowds and keep your virtue,
Or walk with Kings—nor lose the common touch,
If neither foes nor loving friends can hurt you,
If all men count with you, but none too much;
If you can fill the unforgiving minute
With sixty seconds' worth of distance run,
Yours is the Earth and everything that's in it,
And—which is more—you'll be a Man, my son!

✓✗Boundaries✓✗

October 30, 2018

I have taken a sage friend's advice and decided to write about boundaries today. The topic itself is limitless but as I write just about human behaviour and quirks, I might as well deal with it, my way.

Boundary as defined by the dictionary is the greatest possible degree of something or the line or plane indicating the limit or extent of something.

I want to speak about the ambit of human giving, be it emotionally, physically, economically or spiritually.

We are all aware of Daanveer Karna from the epic Mahabharat. No one, as giving as him, has ever walked the face of Earth, it is believed. He never thought what it would cost him to give up what a seeker sought. His ability, of selflessly pleasing every demand made of him, is legendary. Those were simpler times, moreover such men exist in mythology. Drawing a parallel are the Indian women of years gone by. Steeped in customs and bound by social norms, they never thought of their own needs and being. Their lives revolved around the men in their families – fathers, brothers, husbands & sons.

It is not the same nowadays. Thankfully, it is not the same. God has created human beings to be equal and hence our emotional and psychological requirements remain the same no matter what gender we are born with. Today, more than any other time, we need to set our boundaries.

Anyone who has been in love knows that boundaries don't generally apply to certain relationships. Won't we do anything for our parents? If we are closely knit with our siblings, there is nothing we won't do to take them out of a tight corner. Our lives are so entwined with those of our friends that we recognise it as our responsibility to give them anything in our power to make them feel better. Our partners, better halves & romantic interests get the best part of us. Anything that's ours is theirs for the taking.

I feel committing wholeheartedly to any relationship is a very special thing and mostly we have our Rubicons or points of no return. We cannot go back to being what and how we were with somebody, once we cross that line. Once we reach that plane, our happiness and sorrow, our mood swings all depend on the person we are in love with. They basically have the remote control of our lives with them. If they are happy, we are elated. If they are down in the dumps, we keen over too or sometimes we try and pull them out of the pit they find themselves in. All in all, they become the centre of our very being. This situation isn't fair to either party. There might be a thousand different things happening to us, requiring our attention but we always prioritise them over everything else.

Everything takes a backseat when the axis of our lives is in doldrums.

love yourself

MORE.

We consider all this normal. That's how families have always been. That's how romantic relationships have fared through time. That's how human beings show that they care. I am no different. This happens with each one of us.

Having agreed to all the above, I would reiterate the wisdom of many these days, that self-love is important too. The longest relationship we have had or are going to have is with our own selves. No one, absolutely no one can be with us from the start to the finish. All that stays with us is our own body, heart and soul. The least we can do for ourselves, then, is to pay attention. We cannot keep ignoring what pleases us, just in order to keep others happy, however close they might be. I know once we reach the point of no return, it is difficult to think of ourselves first, to peel our attentions from nurturing, caring and tending to others and look after ourselves. It may sound downright selfish too but we cannot pour from an empty cup.

Self care is important. Healing is important. To put ourself first, is important. It's only when we are strong, decisive and whole that we can care for others. So boundaries are important. Setting boundaries don't make us less compassionate. Infact if you feel miserable, depleted and used then that compassion is killing you. We can have compassion for others without actually losing ourselves in the process. Saying no, when you really want to say it, is all right. Saying 'it is fine' when it isn't is not okay.

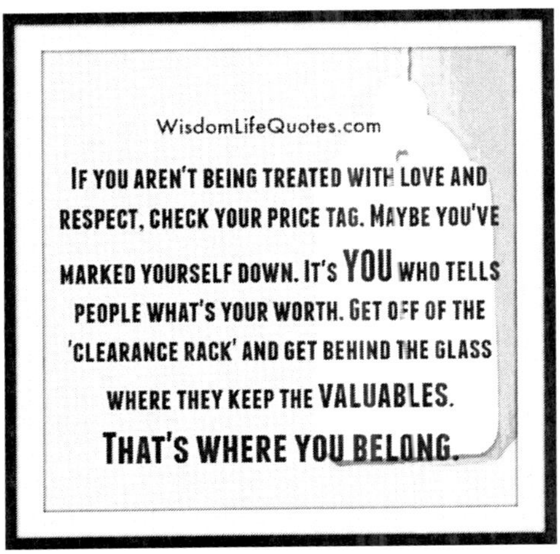

One has to draw a line, erect a wall, not to keep people out but to protect oneself from the blows. Blows that inevitably come when we love or interact with someone. Setbacks, quarrels, disagreements, different opinions, misunderstandings are all a part of this life. They may test one's reserve, they may try one's commitment but they rarely end a true relationship. These are just hiccups. But even while going through them one has to care for oneself. If there is less happiness and more compromise at the end of this trial phase then it is preferable to make your distance, lick your wounds and move on. We don't have to tell the people we love that we care. We won't have to try and make them believe that we do. They would know it and they would acknowledge it and reciprocate and that's when we know that compromises are okay too if at the end we feel loved and recognised.

Trusting Energies!

March 3, 2019

Energy doesn't lie..

I have waited for a week or so, since this realisation hit, to write it all down. I am not an expert on this branch of thinking, I just write what I experience so my account may not be statistically correct. It is at best a point of view, not a point of reference. Having given the disclaimer, I now feel free to share what has been brewing in my mind.

In my humble opinion, people, places, events, plans everything has energy. That energy might be good or bad, positive or negative, dynamic or stagnant, but it does have an impact. We tend to rejuvenate after a vacation or a change of scenery. We can radically change our mood in the company of people- friends or strangers. We alter our perspectives and opinions when we come across fresh persuasive take on things. We react when we are challenged by a new work atmosphere or work profile. That reaction might either be growth or our lack of adaptation. The result doesn't really matter here. All I am trying to say is that energy of a place, people or an event has the potential to change us as human beings–for better or for worse, that depends on myriad factors.

I have known families who have packed up and moved out to new cities because they were not doing as well in their home towns. People change houses all the time and all of us, whether with a conventional outlook or not, believe that the energy of the house would have repercussions on the quality of life of a family. If we move to a new place and fall ill, most people would say that the new house or city didn't suit us. Some might also recommend elaborate religious rites to purify and make the place more conducive to living.

It doesn't take super human powers to get a grip on how these energies work. We, humans, have been endowed with intelligence and logical thinking. More often than not, we realise in the initial stages whether a relationship, a job, a move to a new place, an arrangement, a marriage, a treatment is working or not. But as humans we have also been given an element of hope (the biggest evil to come out of Pandora's box) and a belief in perseverance. We don't leave things or give up on them if they don't work out initially. We just keep at it, hoping it would change.

This is the approach I have an issue with. In my experience, anything that we have misgivings about even before starting out or in the initial stages, doesn't really improve with time and effort. We may feel that it has started working if we see a relative difference in the state of things. It may be due to one of two reasons- the realisation may be due to our own efforts and would cease to exist once we stop putting that input, or the change may well be in the way we look at things, that again would be our own adaptability or acceptance of things as they are.

I know there may be varied views on this. As I said, we are taught to be adaptable. We are told that things would not always be according to our comfort or wishes but we trudge along. That's the way the world has always moved. Nothing wrong with that opinion. To each his own. But for the few who live by the maxim of YOLO, or who feel personal happiness and contentment is important to keep others around us happy, adaptability, as in compromise, is not acceptable.

No one is infallible and if we fall into this trap of disregarding the energies that surround us, we are not naive. We are just what our decent upbringing has made us but expecting happiness in such a scenario would be a little too much to ask. Speaking from experience, I would reiterate that when it comes to people in our lives– whether they are parents, siblings, friends, better halves or romantic interests– we ignore the energies and go about the old fashioned way. We persevere. We hope. We put in an effort. We come to terms with how things will be. That, in most cases, robs us of our peace of mind, our carefree attitude. We refuse to acknowledge 'the energy' of our relationship. We turn a blind eye because what else can we do?

This may not apply to many but holds true for me- When I go to consult a doctor, no matter how accomplished he/she might be or however highly recommended, I cannot put my trust in them if I don't get a positive vibe. I rely on energies. I can't remember the number of opportunities I have had to let go because I cannot work for someone whose aura doesn't draw me in. Miraculously, I don't regret any of those decisions. I am confident that I wouldn't have been content had I compromised.

I have also observed a shift in the energy with the giving up of certain habits, routines, places and people. It is rare that if one huge part of our lives is in turmoil, due to our insistence on holding on to something or someone, another part would flourish. No, it won't. The negative impact of such a vibe would block all the good that other aspects of our life could have. And if at all there is an ouster of this negative energy, everything else also starts falling into place. The moment we decide that we have to get out of a situation that is holding us back, we start to grow and recover. We don't have to go down guilt trip just because we ended something to improve our own lot. We don't have to explain or justify our actions to people who would criticise us any which way. We are here to lead our lives to the best of our abilities. We are not here to please others. Keeping our own selves happy isn't being selfish.

Lighten up. Trust the Energies. Make your own path. It isn't necessary that the well- trodden one is the right way to go. Infact there isn't any right or wrong here, just choices.

As Robert Frost rightly said –

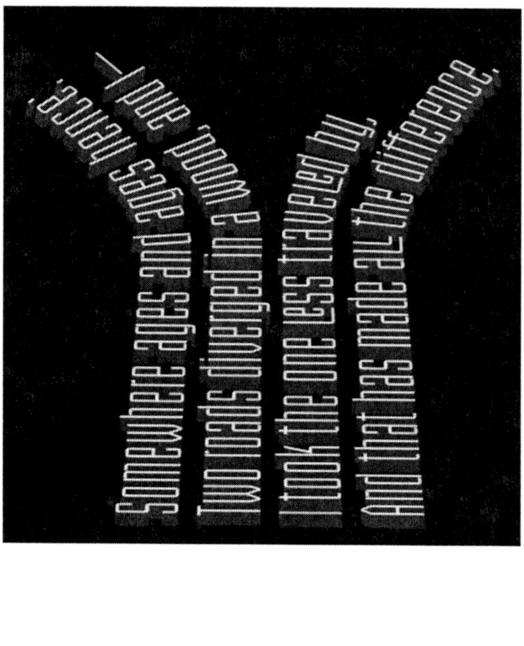

Chaos.. And the Calm!

June 2, 2019

Chaos! Chaos! Chaos!

We hear the word and a visual, a mental image comes up! Something that is helter-skelter, without a set pattern, disorganised, broken, shattered, full of din, mayhem.. Almost violent!

That has been my state of mind, more or less, since I last took to writing. So many things have happened. I have tried escaping it all by every mean possible for me- leaving the place, shunning people, postponing discussions, avoiding confrontations. Gradually I realised, escape doesn't do it. It has to be faced headlong.

Life has taken to dull monotony after the initial shock of things. I would say, the chaos has settled down a little. I have tried making peace with certain aspects, some are still a thorn in the side, but that's life. That's what was written. That's, may be, what I chose, voluntarily or by accident.

I have read a lot in this writing-less span. Not many things have stayed with me, though. It is natural not to retain much when things don't know where to find a home in one's brain. But something that I keep coming back to, is a small piece by a fellow blogger where he speaks about time stamps. It is a beautiful write up and something that I wish I had written. I specifically liked it when he wrote that "Happiness is like a glass of wine, it doesn't last until you have a big bottle of it hidden somewhere."

How true! Sometimes even in the most loving relationships, happiness runs out despite that huge bottle. We forget to refill it. We neglect to stock it. We prefer to ignore it. We take it for granted until, ofcourse, it disappears. And then we run after it, we want it back as it was, we try looking for shared memories but alas, once lost the same isn't available! It is not a consumer good offered at attractive schemes in the market.

There are variants ofcourse. But that's just plain 'settling for less'. I'd rather look for something completely different instead of making do with the chaotic pieces that threaten to loosen up anytime life jolts them again.

Poets have written reams about the beauty of nature after the storm. The green looks all the more greener, the landscape purged of its grime, the debris all settled into new forms, the sun shines brighter on the newly formed tableaux. The character of the land changes, so does its shape and look.

Same goes for the humans who have had to deal with something life- altering like that. The vista is all new for the one's who kept their own through it all.

I have changed. Unapologetically so! Looking forward to the rest of my life. Bring it on! After all, don't the most beautiful rainbows appear after the storms?

Rebels, Misfits & Shattered Souls

June 22, 2019

My mother always says that the character of an individual can be gauged only when you live with them as truly as purity of gold can be measured only on testing it..

"सोने के कसने से और इंसान के बसने से पता चलता है..."

True, may be!

But energies don't work that way. There is some kind of hidden attraction that makes us want to talk to someone or know them better. In my 39 years, I have known many people and have friends from different walks of life.

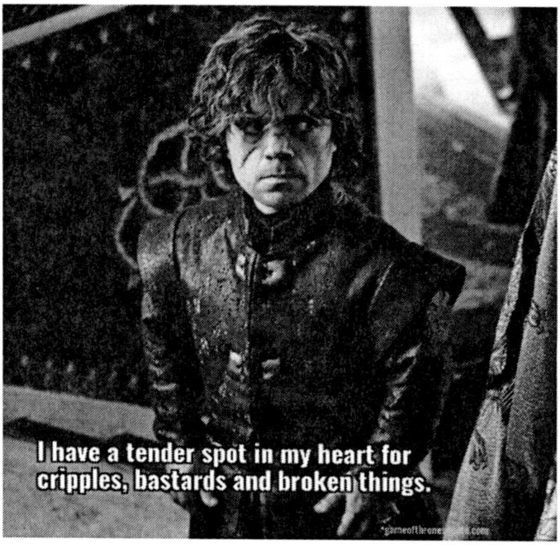

No two people are alike, no one is the same person they were when I first met them. I, myself, have grown into the person I am, due, mainly, to my acquired opinions and experiences. I am sure people who knew me 20 years back would be surprised, if they meet me today.

GROWTH is inevitable. Life puts us through the paces and we learn. If we don't, we stagnate and that is not good for us and for the people around us.

In a mood for self-reflection, I was pleased to realise that among many flaws, that humans inevitably possess and pile up over time, I have developed two of the greatest virtues – First, I don't judge people by their appearances neither do I make my opinions based on first encounters, good or bad. Second, I try not to meddle in the affairs of other people, however close. Infact this, being close and thus a well-wisher, argument doesn't go down well with me at all. I consider these two my paramount achievements in the quest for being a better person.

Having said that, my energies attract a certain kind of clientèle, if you may call them that. Long before Tyrion Lannister made it popular, I have been gravitating towards the troublesome trio of Rebels, Misfits & Shattered Souls. He had a tender spot for cripples, bastards & broken things. I, too, like the ones who are crippled by the choices they made or the ones made for them, bastardized by circumstances and broken beyond repair.

I particularly love the ones who hide their vulnerability behind masks of confidence and straightforwardness. Some might think them to be rude, impolite & uncultured. I find them fascinating. People are not born that way. I, invariably, have this exacting need to find out what made them, the person they are! It gives me immense satisfaction to peel back the layers and uncover the core they are made of.

People haven't disappointed me, so far!

I may have had some lessons along the way but none that I regret. I have had the good fortune of getting to know some exceptional souls hidden behind the veneer of Rebels and Misfits.

They do not conform to the norms. They dress a certain way, speak a certain lingo, act as if they don't give a damn and are willing to, in fact, find pleasure in not being understood by the people around them. They are easy to shun, actually. It is simpler to label them as rebels or misfits and then ignore them.

But what I have found underneath are myriad variety of gems. Some insecure in their abilities, others in their looks and appearances, still others in the circumstances of their lives-social or financial. Some hide their grief beneath all the verve, others are lonely and misunderstood behind the joie de vivre. It is all a facade. And I count myself lucky to be able to bring down the walls, they have erected, brick by brick and know these people as no one around them does.

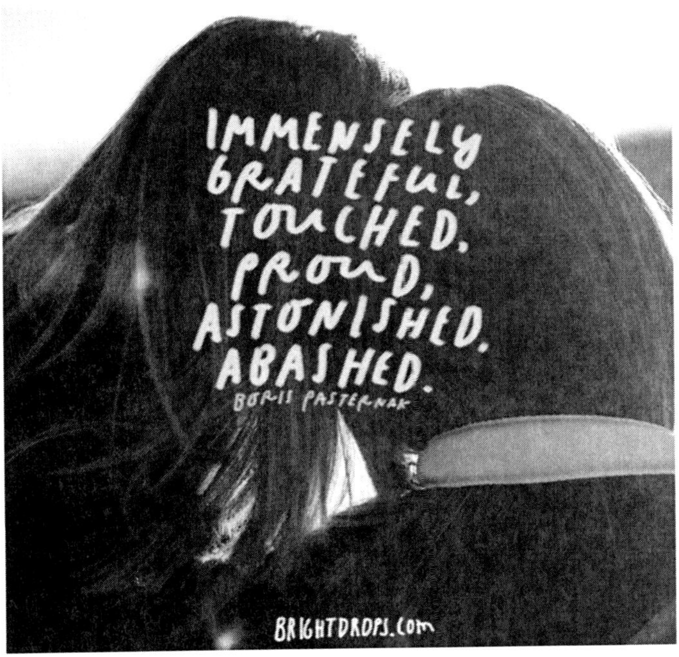

I pride myself on being the unmistakable confidante of many such golden souls and I like to believe that there is always a reason why we meet the people we do. It is as much their healing as mine, and it is all planned by a power that we can't fathom.

Well, grateful!

All in a day's work

June 24, 2019

Life has been good. God has been kind!

True, there are ups and downs in any life. One may be the tiniest of insects and face challenges or the king of the jungle and yet life may not be smooth. We, as humans, have more faculty to deal with problems that come our way because God has bestowed upon us the power to think, analyse and then act accordingly. So, all in all, when I look at my life objectively, I don't find things to complain about, not even the ones that bother me because in the larger picture, the blessings far outnumber the trials.

I have made it a habit to be grateful for whatever I have, small or big. That has given me contentment. The fact that regrets are out, makes me see people and events as experiences. Some might be good, others bad. Who cares! As long as we learn from them.

Out of the many things that I feel grateful for, the most important it seems, is the chance to feel and witness the extraordinary things that ordinary people might do. I have been fortunate to have worked in an atmosphere where rarely did I see people shirking their duties. Everyone was dedicated to the institute and the work culture was relaxed yet disciplined. Nobody needed to be told twice. A task once entrusted was sure to be completed without a hitch, and if there was one, it was solved by putting our heads and energies together. No wonder I remember and miss that place even seven years after leaving it. The people I met there have become mine for life.

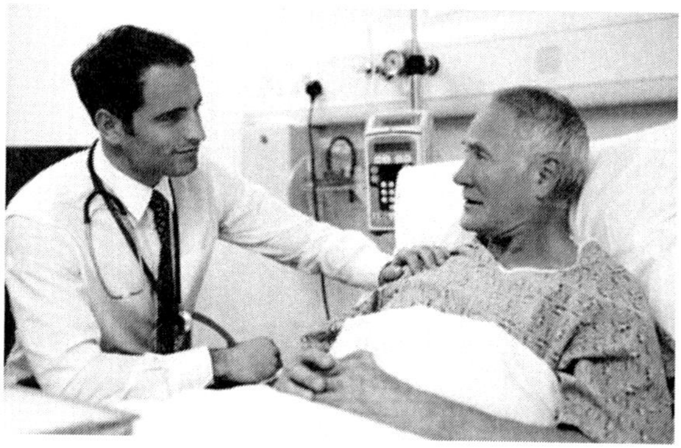

Such is the charisma of great team work when everything moves like a well-oiled machine. I thought that is a rare phenomenon. We couldn't expect the same ambience everywhere we go but I was pleasantly surprised to come across nearly the same energy in the most unexpected of places.

My father was recently diagnosed with chronic kidney disease and after months of battling it with drugs, he is now on dialysis. We live in a small town but we have a state- run dialysis centre in the government hospital here. We were told it was good and moreover it would be convenient for us because we had to go there twice a week. I had seen how state-run things were managed in other sectors and hence was apprehensive. After all it wasn't a one time thing we were getting into.

What I hadn't expected to find, was a team that any organisation could be proud of. Led by a young yet exceptional doctor, these people make things look so easy.

Their camaraderie is reassuring. They are polite, humble and hard working. I sit there for four hours, twice a week and observe them deal with panic situations with a calm that belies some of their ages too. There is nothing more magical than watching ordinary humans turn into paragons of virtue & goodness by dint of their knowledge and confidence in their training.True, they must be working there for years now but that hasn't made them complacent. In fact, I had not seen a more patient, meticulous bunch of healthcare workers, until I met them. Each one is so adept at his or her work. They seem to have each other's back as they carry out the same tedious and monotonous tasks day in and day out. And they do it with a smile on their faces and a spring in their steps.

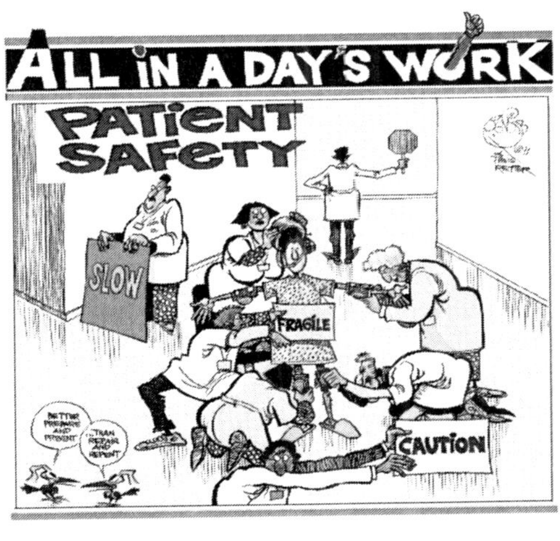

I see them transforming into heroes everyday. Their countenance changes, it becomes shiny and sparkly. There is a confidence in their gait that allays the fears of their patients and a light in their eyes that says- We are here. I cannot help but smile with them. Their energy is contagious. All they want to do is help people. They do everything possible to minimise the suffering of their charges and what is most commendable is that their trainings have made them humble. The impact that their empathy and compassion have on a patient is enormous. An easy smile does it for us.

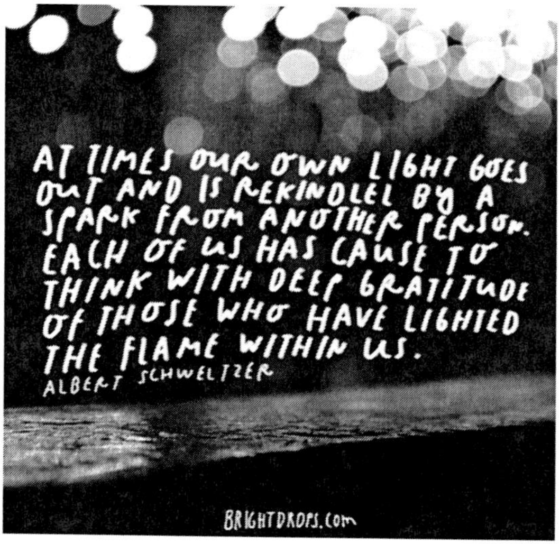

Something that could have been a harrowing experience, if the health care providers couldn't care less, has turned out to be pleasant. I won't say that we look forward to these two days of the week but these people and their mastery over their skills have definitely made it worthwhile.

They won't read it, I know. But I am grateful to them for being themselves. For them, it is all in a day's work, for us it is a debt that cannot be repaid. May God bless them with good health always.

To be or not to be... FREE

June 26, 2019

I went to watch Kabir Singh a couple of days back and since then I have been itching to write this but have been apprehensive. I am a non-confrontational person and I know, I would have to answer my fair share of questions after I put my thoughts in writing. What gave me courage to finally sit down and write are the makers and actors of this movie. Surely, they would have been aware of the backlash they might have to endure when the film, they had so painstakingly made, hit the theatres.

After all, Indians, in general, are a sensitive audience specially when it comes to moral issues.

Thankfully, there wasn't a politicised scene about or reaction as to the impact of a movie like this but the reviews said it all. There were people who said that the moral compass of the makers face duly south to have come up with and endorsed such an idea, some praised the performances and yet disliked the message, the constant refrain is – 'what is the world coming to?' or the young would emulate the character..

It is a classic case of the chick and the egg. What came first? Cinema shows what is happening in the society, it is a mirror of what we see around or is it cinema that gives birth to unconventional ideas and air them for innocent, unknowing people to emulate? We can't blame the makers for making something that is already rampant in the society. It is our denial mindset which fails to acknowledge that this, in fact, is the reality in modern day India.

And come to think of it, what part of the movie do we not see around? If it is a negative, toxic relationship we have aversion to then it isn't all that rare. In fact, it is more common than the common cold. Always has been. There have been other films too that have portrayed this toxicity and let's face it, we do see it in everyday life too. The boy obsessing over the girl and the girl eventually giving in to the care and attention, overlooking the toxic behaviour, is an everyday phenomena. Most couples realise it later when the initial flush of love and sex wanes. I was amazed at the female character, though. Where do we find such demure girls nowadays? And that too someone hailing from a metro city.

There are instances of alcohol and drug abuse (I am calling it abuse because the boy nearly kills himself with an overdose) in the movie along with excessive smoking. Now, all these have long been considered evils in the society and also a threat to one's health. But has that stopped anyone from using them? They are openly available in the market. They are addictions and thus the manufacturers and governments know that people will buy them, come what may. I should be candid in saying that they are in fact a major source of income to the government, through the taxes. It is not that the young would start smoking, drinking or resorting to drugs if they fail in love. The modern day Devdas is a myth. People drink and smoke because they want to. It has always had this added image quotient of 'looking cool with it', attached to it.

Anger issues and a devil may care attitude which the male lead portrays is not to give a certain edge to the character, it is in fact a flaw that many of us are dealing with. As a teacher, I have seen it a lot in the students of a certain age. Some mellow down, others don't. The language used also has become an everyday part of our lives. The abuses that are hurled around, the gaalis are something that the young don't even notice because they have been using them for years now. Some of them have actually become terms and phrases of endearment among friends.

If it is the operating or performing surgery under influence or ethics of a doctor that worry an audience, then it has been dealt with convincingly in the film. The character, himself, takes the moral high ground by accepting that he is an alcoholic and that although he hasn't brought any harm to any of his patients till date yet he would take the punishment or penalty of putting them into danger by merely handling them in such a state.

The content of the movie was a surprise to me, because rarely have Hindi movies been so explicit in dialogue, language, wit, state of undress and mannerism. There is no inhibition in asking for sex or 'physical help', as the actor puts it or counting the number of times that a couple has been intimate with each other or, for that matter, the hero explaining to his dad the meaning of 'personal space' reminding him that he, the father, had got married at the age of 23 and he, his son is still unmarried at 28. So, he should actually understand what personal space between a girl and a boy would mean. Some might find it bold but the boy also confronts the girl's father when he catches them kissing on the terrace saying that had they been married and he been his son-in-law, the father would have walked off giving them that space. For the first time, I saw an acceptance of the physical part of any romantic relationship, not only in the characters of the movie but also in the raucous crowd of spectators gathered there.

I was surrounded by a youthful crowd during the movie and they bawled and hooted as much on the intimate scenes as they did on the sudden appearance of a bearded and cool-looking hero or his motorbike, for crying out loud. I did not hear any gasps of surprise or scandalous hawws from the audience on such scenes. The idea wasn't alien to them, atleast not to most of them. I found myself laughing with them. I am middle-aged, to say the least, but I could appreciate the wit embedded in the dialogues too.

All because it is a Hindi movie, the makers had to give it a happy ending and that was my only disappointment. It was unconventional and yet so refreshing when the hero doesn't even blink an eyelid when he sees the pregnant heroine and it comes naturally to him. It is not even a question in his mind. He has already accepted the child as it is her flesh and blood, not bothering about where the sperm came from! But then to appease the moral sensibilities of the audience, who cannot be kept out even with an 'A' certification, the makers twisted the story and Indianised it. It was, infact, their love child she was carrying and she had been living on her own all these months.

Barring this minor hiccup, I had fun watching the movie and I loved the performance of Shahid Kapoor and am totally taken in with the music of the film.

May more such movies be made without the fear of them corrupting the society. If we believe that such movies corrupt the society and if the impact of a movie can be so obvious then why don't we improve as a society when we see virtues there? Why don't we emulate the good? A movie is a movie. The purpose of its creation is telling a tale, entertaining people, and ofcourse raking in the moolah, for it is business too. Let's not place the responsibility of making or breaking a generation squarely on its shoulders. The decadence of a society isn't solely due to its art, but its art does reflect what is seen in the society.

We have already stepped into the 21st century and made our individual decisions as to how we want to lead our lives. What a person does in his or her personal life shouldn't be a cause for moral policing, judgement or interference by anyone.

There is a dialogue in the movie that 'one should not be so free-willed in a democracy'. I think it is time to challenge that!

🥰On Connections🥰

August 21, 2019

Human relationships are so weird. Rarely, are people satisfied with their lot in life. We have a mental checklist of what would appeal to us and what will fulfill us. More often than not, we don't actually find what we are looking for, in a friend or a partner. And sometimes, just sometimes, it all falls into our lap even when we are not actively looking for it.

As a free-thinking and independent woman, what I want in a relationship are deep set values, compatibility, my kind of humour, resourcefulness and a charm that would bind me, would make me feel 'that special flutter' within. Good looks are objective.

I have often come across the question of love at first sight and I have constantly believed that it doesn't happen. You cannot love a person just because he or she is easy on your eyes. Love might not happen that way but connections do happen.

Sometimes there is a certain energy between two people that binds them even at first sight. Try as we might, we cannot stay away from such cosmic energy. There is a reason why people come into our lives. They might not tick all our boxes but with such people we need no further reason to stay. We don't even have to try very hard. It just falls into place. Effortlessly. That's how great Friendships are forged. There is no rationality to it. Rationality in the eyes of the society, I mean. People ask questions that go from 'how can you trust someone in such short a period?' to 'will it not create an imbalance in your already existing relationships?' Some even feel that just because one has been friends with someone for a longer period of time, one has to prioritize them. But human relationships do not grow like that. Certain things are just unexplained.

I have a couple of unexplained relationships in my life. Whatever these two people might do, I can't stay upset with them for long. I love them both, deeply, in their own unique ways. One is like a progeny to me another a very good friend and interestingly both these connections happened at our very first meetings. There were no denials or dilly-dallying about the nature of our relationship. What these two give me is a feeling of contentment without any hassles. There are no major differences of opinions. Both these men listen to what I have to say and reserve their judgements. They give me space to think, act and have my own opinion on things. Interestingly, both have a very wide world view. They never categorise life and its decisions into just right or wrong. What may be wrong for you, might make all the sense to someone else, is their mantra. I have seen them apply it in their lives and stay happy with the decisions and choices they make. This ability inspires me. It is rare to find even one such connection in life and I have been blessed with two.

May they always stay the same, wherever they go. May they always keep touching lives like they have touched mine. Exceptional people that they are, may they continue to find peace and contentment in the years to come.

I know neither of them would read it, nonetheless, this piece. They already know how I feel about them and they won't need words to validate it.

Anchors

August 26, 2019

When I was a kid I used to find it funny when, at family gatherings to celebrate the birth of a child, all adults would gush to the beaming parents that the child takes after one or both of them. 'He has the exact same nose', 'she smiles just like you', 'look at the forehead, she takes after her grandpa', on and on the comparisons went and it was funny to me because a new born looked more like a Primate than a person to me.

As I grew up a little, I realised that babies and puppies are mostly always cute, no offence. Now, where, I could pick up and cuddle a puppy, I couldn't do the same with babies. So, ofcourse, I loved puppies more it seemed.

My younger sister is about five years my junior and it would have been quite logical to develop those feelings of affinity and love when she was born but I was a jealous little prick back then and the only thing that her birth could mean to me was that my father's attention would be shared now.

So my maternal instincts did not come to the fore until my most loved nephew was born in 2001. By then, I had been in the teaching line for a couple of years and, even then, I wasn't comfortable surrounded by the kindergarten lot. I just couldn't handle the tiny humans. I could relate to kids only after a certain age when they could hold their own in a conversation and understand the flow of words.

With age, I have learnt to portray an acceptable level of tolerance for the kids in the family but I still can connect with just three of them- my nephews and an extremely bright niece, who is just seven but seems to be 17 when she argues. These three, too, are more my friends than kids. They call me by my name as I have taught them to and interact with me as if I am a year or two younger than them.

Some would say that this, lack of motherly traits, is what has kept me away from 'holy matrimony' and the kids that follow but I just don't care what people say and how they react to this. Having said that, the truth is that I did not get married and I don't have kids of my own.

I wish I could say that it has been a loss, only if to appease the majority. But I don't see it that way. I don't feel a void in this case because of these three and an extremely important connection with someone who calls me Maa. The four of them have tethered my heart to their own and are my anchors, my reasons to live and carry on despite the struggles. They represent Hope to me. If there is genuine happiness in the world, I get it from this foursome and if there is a selfless bone in my body, I have it for these four children.

A friend of mine keeps quoting a punjabi saying "Apne hi baal te apniyaan hi maawaan" which, loosely translated, means that only the kids, you have given birth to, are your own and that one can neither become a mother to someone who isn't her flesh and blood, nor can a child be as attached to someone who isn't his or her biological mother.

I have always differed to agree on this. I don't know what the future has in store for me. Sayings become popular for a reason. It is possible that at some point in their lives these four precious parts of my heart would choose something or someone I would not be susceptible or predisposed to. But I am prepared for that. After all, it is their life and after a certain point they are entitled to take decisions for their own good. These choices may or may not be acceptable to all the people in their lives. That in no way means that they would love me less. It would only mean that, with me, they would have the liberty to choose what their hearts really want.

I have no idea what good parenting is. I used to feel that having a kid means to have a person who is completely yours for life, someone who is one hundred percent yours and yours alone because you have given life to that being. But it doesn't happen that way with your biological progeny too. What I have learnt is to control myself from holding them back. My heart bleeds when I see my children going down a path that would bring them grief but I have learned from my own life that no amount of convincing and cajoling would deter them from a chosen path just because a parent's wisdom says so. Hence, it is judicious to let them make their own mistakes and learn from them. Lessons thus learnt would stay with them longer.

And years later, may be or may be not, some casual observer would say, look at them, they take after you in all but looks. Wouldn't that be the happiest day of my life?

✨Purpose✨

November 30, 2019

For as long as I can remember, I have been an atheist. I have no particular grouse with God. Life has been largely good and comfortable for me. It is just that the whole concept of religion as propounded by man confounds me. Not one to argue, I chose to just not believe in HIM yet steering clear of the confrontation. That makes me more of an agnostic I guess.

I have encountered people with unwavering faith in God, people who would continue to believe even when odds are stacked against them, people who would smile through the pain and say if it is God's will there must be something good in it. I have marvelled at such people and the resilience of their characters.

Like the young Buddha when he was still Siddharth, I was cocooned by my parents too and thus didn't know much about suffering. My compassion for others was acquired through a lot of reading and was basic, to say the least. There comes a time in every human's life when life starts throwing curve balls and we have to use all the skills at our disposal to deal with them. Siddhartha understood hunger, old age, misery and death when he saw them first hand but then he was an enlightened and evolved soul, so was quicker to realisation than me.

I prided myself in staying strong and dry- eyed even in the face of death. I have seen a lot of people go and have maintained a resolute stance through it all. It did move me but not to the core. Cold- hearted was an adjective that my family and friends gave me.

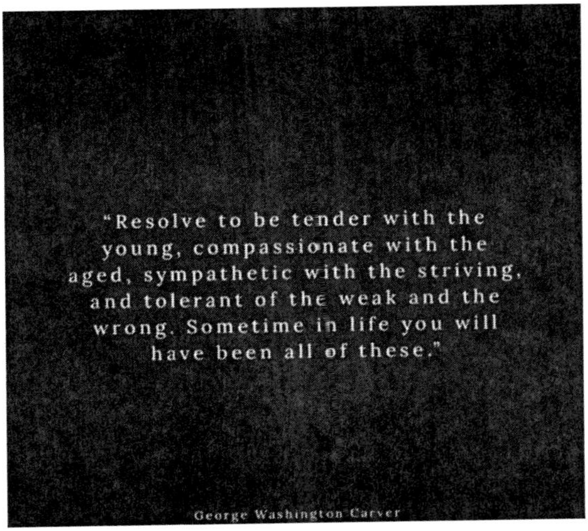

But lately, I have developed a deeper sensitivity of suffering, pain and disease when I encountered them close at home. Watching my father battle through different stages of the chronic kidney disease has given me a new perspective on life. I have come to appreciate the little things, the brief respites, the genuine smiles, the idea of letting go, forgiveness and most of all LOVE, COMPASSION, KINDNESS and CARE– in essence God.

A few days back I came across a picture on one of the social media sites that asked a pertinent question as to what the purpose of one's life was and that most people took living to be just breathing, eating, earning and spending until they die. To that I say, each day life and the people around us teach us something new. Our lives are God's way to evolve our souls by grinding into them the virtues of love, tenderness, compassion, patience and stoicism.

These days, more often than not, I find myself tearing up at the suffering that other patients go through on our visits to the dialysis centre. I am filled with gratitude towards God that we have had a whole and healthy life and that dad has taken ill only at this age in his life. I see children of 6,7,10,18 years of age going through dialysis with nothing but a bleak future ahead. Organ transplant isn't an option for them with the high costs involved.

I have learnt everyday from the smiling health care professionals who are there to see us through any complication or phase that raises its ugly head. I have seen them bear the brunt of anger, frustration and helplessness of their patients and still go about their work with nary a crease on the brow. There have been times when I have broken down under stress, uncertainty and the burden of decision- making and yet one word or conversation with the dialysis staff has been enough to calm my mind and allay my fears. I bow down to their spirit and the hope that they represent.

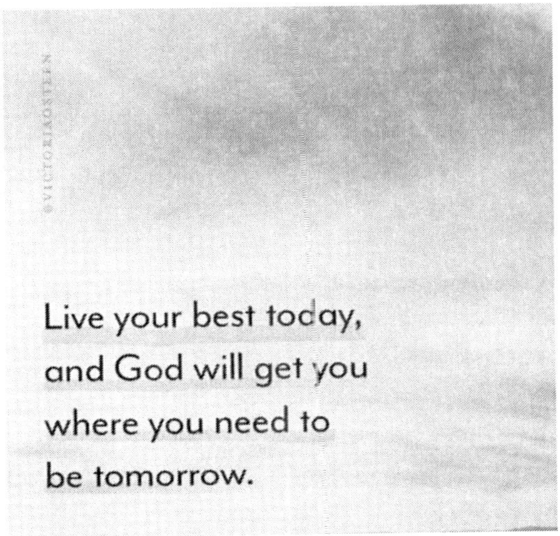

I still don't go to a temple but nowadays, I pray. And I thank HIM everyday for the blessings that I have been taking for granted all my life. I thank HIM for the people he has sent to enrich my life and to help me get through it. I don't ask for anything, not out of pride, just because I don't see HIM as the fulfiller of wishes but as a wise guide who is teaching me every step of the way. If I walk the path laid down for me to the best of my abilities, may be, there would be contentment at the end.

Parts of You

January 15, 2020

Half Agony, Half Hope… That's love♡
The things you eat,
the people you meet.
The places you go,
your music that flows…
The way you swear,
the moments you care..
I have YOU stored in these small parcels, pictures, videos, memories…
for the times eternal that we won't be together,
I will always, always carry a part of you with me.

😌Solace😌

April 16, 2020

An unmarried friend of mine used to extol the virtues of spinsterhood all the time, saying that she would never miss something she hadn't experienced when told that she would miss the company of a partner in her old age. I agreed with her wholeheartedly. I remember telling my father about yet another unmarried friend and her frustration with life saying that, she is frustrated because she wants to get married and hasn't been able to. It is not the same situation as mine.

I was happily single even when there was this guy who loved me with all his heart. I could never feel the passion within. For three long years, we tried to come to even ground. May Lord bless him, he never gave up. But I was done living a lie. There was a time when I had made up my mind to stop looking for what I desired and make do with what I was given. But the only sensible thing I did was not to deceive myself and him. I know, I broke his heart terribly but it would be better for him in the long run.

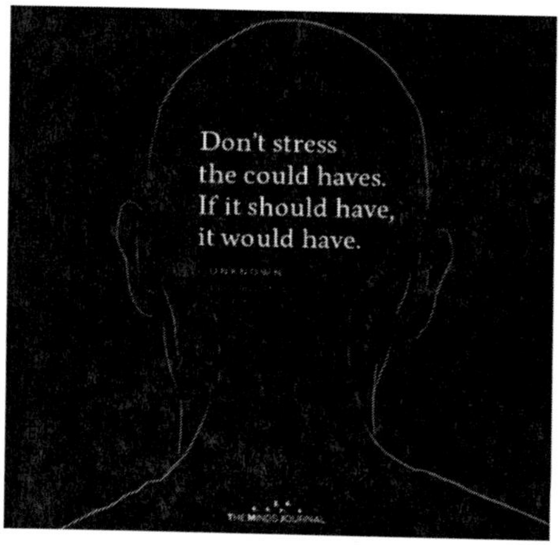

I believe that.

Soon after, I met someone I had been looking for all my life. For me, it was as if lightning struck right from the first moment I laid eyes on him. Why God decided to give me my heart's desire at 39 in a very complicated package? I don't know.

I sit and think sometimes what is it that makes me forgive everything he does, or condone even those of his actions that hurt me. I have always been a thinking individual who has had this quality of self – love deeply ingrained in her, then why this sudden shift where I think of someone else before me?

What makes me do that, which is new to my basic nature and tendencies? It isn't as if this is permanent, infact the premise of our relationship is its temporary nature and yet this need in me to make life easy for him, to be a woman in the relationship.

I came across a line in a movie recently (the movie was poorly made and leaves no other imprint on the watcher). It said, "We like people because and love them despite"

Meaning (as I understood it) – We like people because of their qualities, because of the care they give us, the things they do for us, because we think alike, because we have been thrown together by fate or because we have the same concerns and circumstances in life.

But we love people despite their shortcomings, despite the fact that we are so unlike each other, despite our different upbringing & backgrounds, despite our separate outlooks on life, irrespective of our language, culture and the choices in people and things, sometimes even despite the fact that we have to tread separate paths in life and that we cannot be together per se. We love them for who they are and for what they bring to our life.

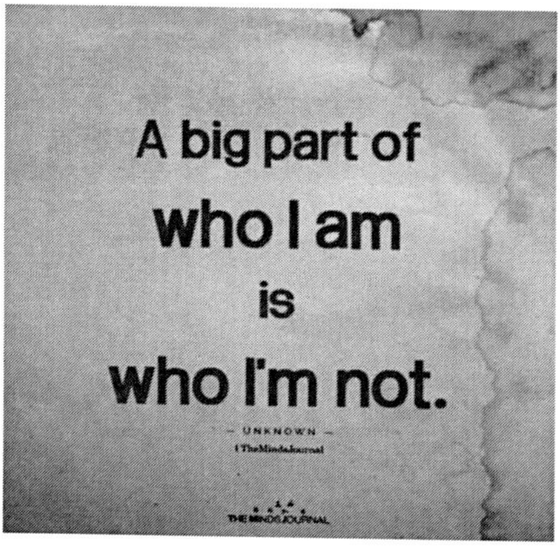

No human being should look for fulfillment in another. I believe if one is not complete on his or her own, they cannot give anything to any kind of relationship. Hence, we have our passions, our hobbies, our friends, our work and our 'me time'. All these things make us happy and content which makes us radiant. And a radiant person attracts others. A person who is, thus self – sufficient, is not clingy because they don't look for completion in any one relationship or job. They are who they are because of the life they have lived or the experiences they have had.

But human relationships do bring an iota of happiness, solace & contentment for us. We feel calmer in the presence of certain people, with some we feel confident, there are a few who provide us with a sense of safety, there are one or two who bring out the real us, we can be our weird selves around some, yet others can make us explore the sides of us which we never knew existed within us.

What if, we find all of this or most of it in one person?

That, sure, screws us up because that's exactly what everyone is looking for in the world. The ultimate human quest. It is not money or the name we make or our social standing, it is the meaningful relationships that keep us going.

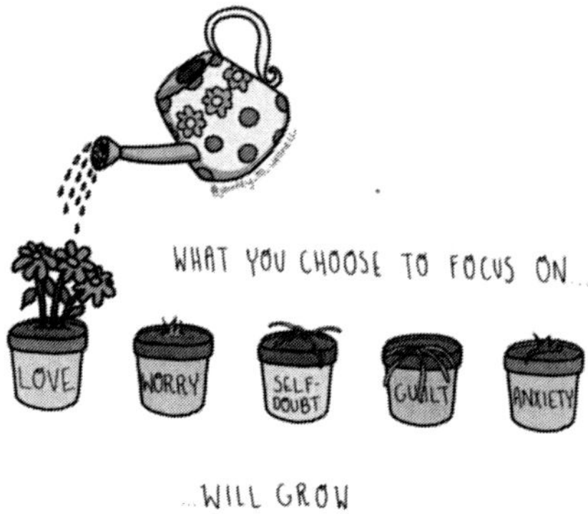

Now, the tragedy of someone like me, who has a wide perspective on life and a hugely open mind, is that we don't want such relationships labelled by the conventional standards of our society. I am not saying that acceptability by the society is too cliché. I am not a rebel for rebels sake. In fact, I have been a dutiful daughter all my life, someone who has put my own happiness at bay just to keep my family name up, to live up to the recognition my father has in the society. It took an immense amount of courage for me to write about it all but it has been eating me up inside, for days. I am not someone who would go against the norms just to prove that I am different or I am above it all.

Obviously, it would be a pleasure, surpassing everything, to be accepted for whoever I am or whoever I love. But my point is, labelling a near perfect thing like the one described above, specially in complicated situations, puts unnecessary pressure on the individuals and all the magic is lost.

So, the answer to my own question, as to why God deemed it fit to introduce me to a person of that kind so late in my life, is that HE wanted me to experience the life HE had given me to the fullest. HE wanted me to absorb this hugely giving feeling of love and compassion. HE wanted life to come full circle for me before it all ended. HE did not want to leave me and my soul in a dismal state before we met HIM finally.

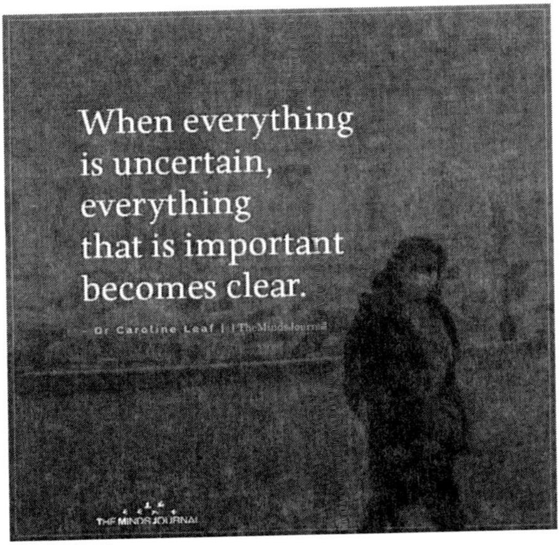

I put my atheism in a sack, tie huge boulders to it and throw it away in the deepest of oceans finally and bow down to his presence and might.

This quarantine has made me realise the important things in life and the importance of accepting the significant parts of life. I might miss his constant presence when our time together is up. I might also miss his physical attributes – his smile, laughter, anger, irritation on my constant repetitions, his smell, touch and the like. I may be desolate and lonely at times too. I am just a human. But, even so, I would be content for having lived this limited time with him. I would want for nothing else.

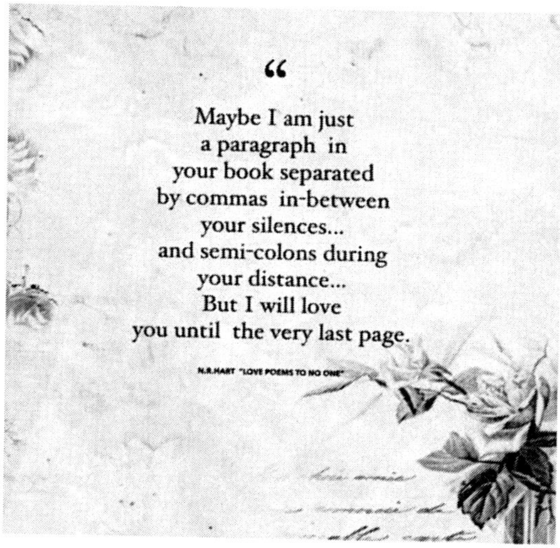

Striking the Balance

April 22, 2020

We learn everyday.

We learn from nearly everyone and everything around us.

We are not the same person as we were yesterday.

We won't be the same as we are today.

Life has a sharp learning curve.

It is not always kind.

Nothing ever goes away without teaching us what it was created to & met us for.

We are beaten into shape by whatever we go through,

just as the huge sharp rocks are rounded by the constantly flowing water.

When does it hurt the most?

I recently read somewhere that when you are sad and hurt, take a breath, sit and ponder what has made you sad. You will find that the thing that brings you immense joy alone has the power to make you sad.

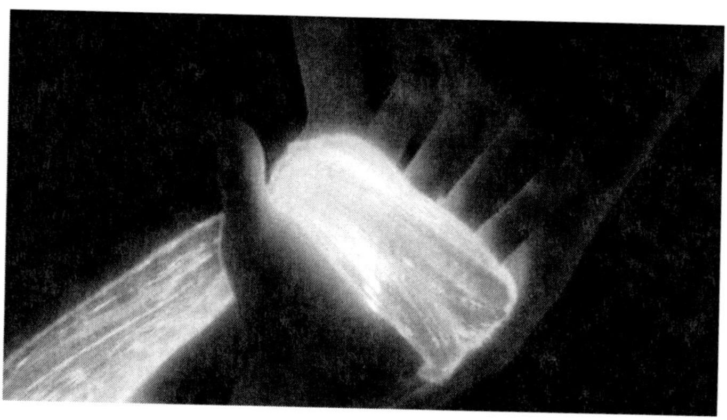

Similarly, when we are happy we should remember that the reason for our happiness might and will bring us grief someday. It is inevitable like day and night.

> When you are joyous, look deep into your heart and you shall find it is only that which has given you sorrow that is giving you joy.
>
> When you are sorrowful look again in your heart, and you shall see that in truth you are weeping for that which has been your delight.
>
> Some of you say, "Joy is greater than sorrow," and others say, "Nay, sorrow is the greater." But I say unto you, they are inseparable. Together they come, and when one sits alone with you at your board, remember that the other is asleep upon your bed. Verily you are suspended like scales between your sorrow and your joy."
>
> ~ Kahlil Gibran

They never remain the same…

Love, Life, Chance or Game

You win some, you lose some

They bring sorrow, at other times fame

Sometimes they wax, soon after, wane.

Let the joy wash over you and accept the pain

There is always a reason it happened as it did,

We are merely pawns and this is HIS grand ballgame.

All we can learn is to treat both up and down just the same.

Of Music & Life🎹 🎶

May 4, 2020

This morning I was listening to an audio book 'Becoming' by Michelle Obama.

Not only is the book absorbing, but her narration is spell-binding too.

In one of her anecdotal episodes, she recounts how she learnt to play the piano from her Aunt. She tells us a little something about pianos. On her very first day, her no- nonsense aunt asked her to put her thumb on Middle C. Now, she was just about six years old then and had no idea what a Middle C was. The piano for her was a wide array of black and white keys which her six year old hands could not reach.

But eventually she found out that Middle C is the anchoring point. It is the point where treble and bass stand divided. She says that if one could manage to put her thumb firmly on the Middle C then everything else falls automatically in place. The right hand knows which keys to press and so does the left.

This got me thinking.. As in music, so it is in life. We just have to find our Middle C for things to fall into place. She had an advantage at her aunt's place. The Middle C key on her aunt's piano was disfigured hence it was easy to place. She practiced and learnt how to play beautifully.

On her first ever recital for the public she came on the stage to find a flawless piano and was in a turmoil because she wasn't used to 'flawless'

Her aunt understood her quandary and pointed out the Middle C, after which she played without a hitch.

It so often happens with us too. We do have elders and more experienced people around us to constantly point out the Middle C in our lives- the point which separates right from wrong, moral from immoral & virtue from vice. But unlike a piano, where the key we are talking about is constant, life does not roll like that.

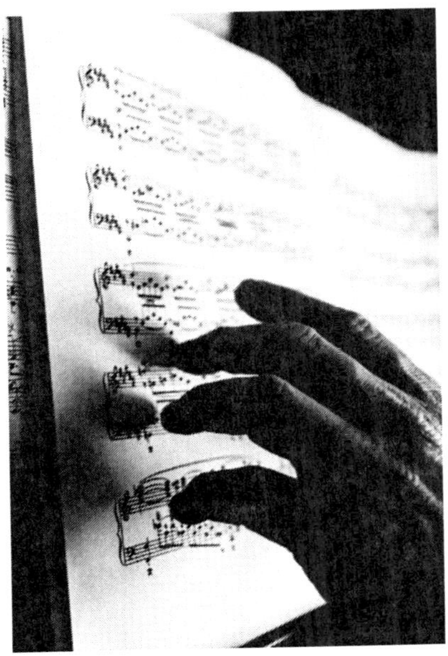

What may be right for one, might be all wrong for someone else. The morality and virtue we talk about is subjective. What works for one may not work for the other. It isn't fair or even realistic to make rules & societal norms, and expect everyone to adhere to them whether or not they feel okay with them.

Our society has a yardstick to measure or judge people. And it is unfortunate that anyone venturing out of those boundaries is considered wayward or obstinate or even a rebel. Be it love, human relationships, work, ambitions, lifestyle – everything has to be within those standards to be accepted by the society.

God hadn't made us like that. We made society to keep us company not to keep us aloof.

I feel, every thinking – person, who has some kind of experience in life or even if they don't, has the right to choose the way they live and love.

All we have to do is find our own Middle C's and carry on with the symphony that this life should be. We should be able to follow our own tunes if they make sense to us. Even if the notes are discordant at first they would fall into harmony, which suits us, soon enough or they would give us an experience that would be hard to forget.

Just a thought!

💜What if💜

May 6, 2020

Lately, when I sit down and ponder
I consistently wonder,
How different it could all have been
Had I met you at a different stage, a different scene!

It is said that there is no what if or if only,
Things are, as they are destined to be.
That, it is all written by God's infallible hand
To doubt it would tempt divine reprimand.

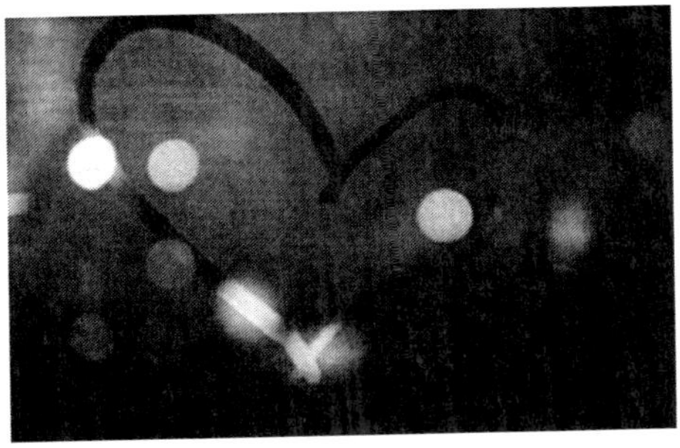

There has been no reason to regret till now
We reap the fruits of whatever we sow.
Yet, just in this case,
I wish I could trade place
With the one who has you, eternally to cherish,

Oh, How I wish!

They say, forever is promised to no one
So I try and make the most of what I have been given.
But this hope refuses to decline
What if I could prompt fate
And call you 'MINE'….

Of Indifference & Love❤

May 15, 2020

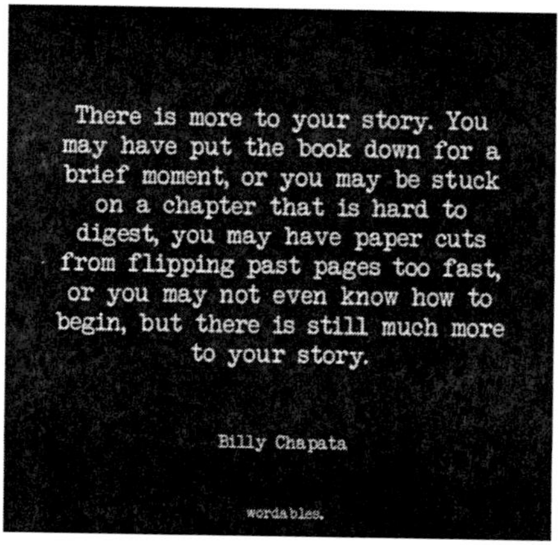

In a quest to get to the bottom of the indifference I, so frequently, see in people these days, I went back some years on the Facebook timelines of some of my more perplexing friends. I was so heartened to find normal college lives, camaraderie with friends, venting of emotions without hesitation, in some cases, even with great aplomb in English that is broken at best, confessions of first loves & first heartbreaks. The honesty of such posts made me smile.

And then, I compared them to the same people I know now. Words fail me– there is a veneer so thick, a mask so snug that they themselves don't realise that they have changed beyond recognition. They are no longer the carefree people they once were.

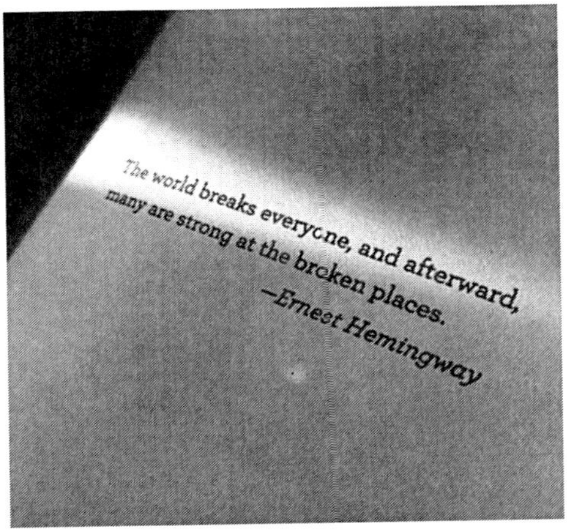

What makes good people change into such versions of themselves where their inherent honesty is buried so deep within that most people they interact with don't even take the trouble of venturing in? And those who do, almost always, are hurt by their indifference and 'it doesn't matter to me either way whether you stay or leave' attitude or 'what is to like in a job as long as it pays the bills' syndrome. This 'made up shell' might be their defence mechanism against the scourge of life but, in my opinion, it keeps them away from more meaningful relationships both personally and professionally. They have made walls that keep people out. These barriers might save them from some hurt along the way but are extremely limiting in the long run.

Don't get me wrong, I am not against change. Infact, I know, no person stays the same over the years. We change with our experiences. We grow. Sometimes we wallow too. This is LIFE. It breaks & remoulds the best of us. There is no human alive who hasn't had his or her fair share of trials, turbulences, grief, heartbreaks & losses but we have also had love, friendships, family, triumphs, happiness and moments to cherish. It is upto us what we act on and become.

Whatever the world might say for them, I prefer people who wear their hearts on the sleeve. They may be considered naive, emotional fools who are susceptible to being hurt but they are honest and they don't have a mask on. All the grief, heartbreak, failure and disappointment haven't made them lose faith in the good things that life has to offer. They haven't become sceptics. They may be annoying or clingy but they are themselves. They don't have to deal with two sides of their own pschye- one who they actually are and the second what they let the world see.

In my experience, people who are indifferent to love or human proximity are the ones who need it the most. They just can't bring themselves to acknowledge it when they have it or admit, even to themselves, the fact that they do need it. They are prepared to lose & suffer rather than accept that they crave love too. They stay in denial. Outward appearances belie the truths inside. They may be the coolest people in a crowd but hollow inside. They may be magnets for people to rally around, eat, drink, socialise and make merry but their connections are mostly always superficial & banal. When they can't accept love, they can't give it away either. After all, we cannot pour from an empty cup, can we? At the end of the day, one has to face oneself. We might not realise our loneliness unless & until we are fair and truthful to ourselves. The most important conversation would be how we answer our own questions when we look ourselves in the mirror. How happy we are, if at all, is how happy we let ourselves be..

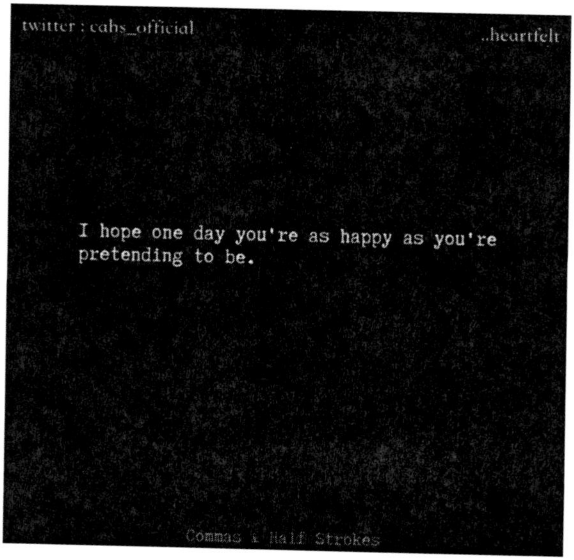

Is it, then, justified to keep ourselves aloof for fear of getting hurt? Is it worth all the trouble to be recognised as cool and detached, when in the end, it might leave us with nothing concrete? Is being emotional so wrong? Can we not still have hope and faith in love and goodness of people despite our bad experiences?

In the end, it is all a CHOICE. Shutting our eyes to dangers doesn't make them go away. It is what pigeons do. They close their eyes and hope that the cat won't see them. It doesn't happen that way in life. It is just that we don't see it coming and when it hits us, it knocks the wind out of us and we get to blame fate, once again. Is it not more prudent, then, to keep one's eyes open and let everything that life has in store for us, in- without fear of repercussions and anticipation of the hurt?

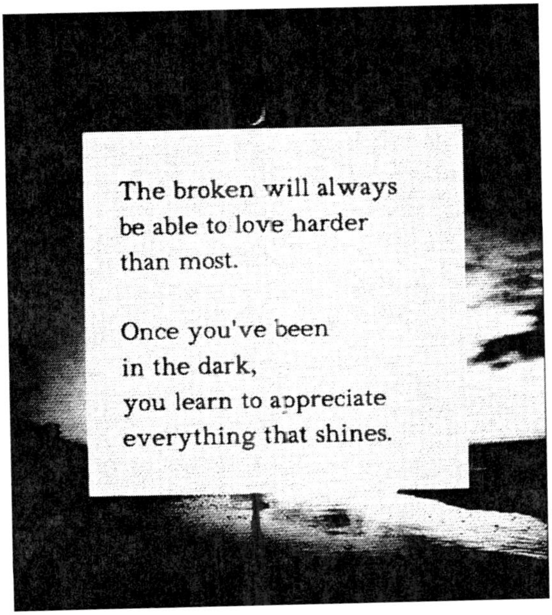

The most content people I have come across are those who accept everything with an open mind and heart, those who have seen and experienced both sides of life without changing the core of their being. They are the influencers not the impressionables. It is all right if we love or hate something with a passion, be it on work or personal front but we should try and make an effort not to be indifferent. It won't be fair to us. We have one life. It isn't proper for us to sit on the fence and let that pass us by, having not lived it one way or the other.

If it doesn't matter, leave it. Move on. Don't stick to it and hurt others too. Be it a job or a relationship. Be there. Either all in or all out. CHOOSE. Don't do things half way.

Just a random thought!

I am an intense person.
I don't do things half way.
I'm all in or all out.
You either have all of me
or you don't get me at all
- IZZY SMITH | TheMindsJournal
THE MINDS JOURNAL

Debt

May 30, 2020

When does the debt end? At what age or point in life or after earning how much money does the debt of a parent end?

🥰♡♡🥰

What I am about to write may not resonate with many but it will echo with the core Indian values we have all been brought up with.

A news in today's newspaper gave me a jolt and I just couldn't understand why it had to happen this way. It was regarding the death of an octogenarian who lived with his seventy five year old paralytic wife. The husband fell down and passed away at night probably due to a stroke or heart failure, the invalid wife dragged herself till the dead body and unable to shout out or seek any help, she kept sitting with the body all night. When the domestic help came in the morning and found the door locked, she sought the neighbour's help and thus found these two in this state- the man dead and his wife unconscious, dehydrated and too weak to even cry.

Apparently, these two have two highly successful sons one of whom lives abroad and the other in a metro. The neighbours maintained that they hardly ever had visitors and even the sons visited rarely.

I don't know the circumstances of their lives nor do I have the right to judge what people do in their lives or how they deal with things that life throws at them, but I found this disturbing. Anything could have happened to two old, invalid people living all alone without a twenty – four hour help or vigilance and IT DID. Isn't it the worst way to go? What would have been going through the mind of the survivor who spent the night looking at the lifeless body of her spouse?

🥰🥰

In the same vein, I am sometimes irked by the undeserved praise that is heaped on me for looking after the health and needs of my father who is on dialysis. I call it ‘undeserved‘ because according to me it is just my duty towards him that I am fulfilling. It doesn’t warranty praise. It is something that we do. We just do it. There is no way around it. There is no one else who would shoulder this responsibility and there is no actual need for anyone else. Our parents raise us to be the people we become. It is their effort and energy that they put into my life that I have an identity. My education, my upbringing and even my initial thought process, everything has come from them. They are the ones who sacrificed their happiness and comfort so that I could get something inconsequential but was important to me at that time. They scraped and saved so that I could have a cushion to fall back on in my hard days. There are people who would come up to me and tell me that I am performing a stellar job managing his health the way I am and that who would miss a son if a daughter can care in such a way (the most insulting thing to say to someone like me).

🥰🥰

All children have this ‘debt‘. Our parents don’t seek repayment, they don’t expect ‘quid pro quo‘, but it is on our conscience. I am not saying that one should not have a life of one’s own. God knows, I do. Even we, as children, have a right to go out, make friends, love, marry, have a family, bag a job, work, earn money- respect-a name of our own in the society, live life the way we deem fit, but our parents- the ones who gave us this life- shaped us- had our backs, should be inclusive in this life, not forgotten or treated like a burden. True, when we live together we have differences of opinion, we have generation gap, we do not agree on everything that our parents hold dear but that's not a reason that love, respect and duty should wane. If we are compromising on our way of life, they are adjusting too- to a new world where they do not control everything as they did in their active lives, to the opinions and lifestyles of their kids who they want to understand but sometimes fail to, to an ever changing belief system, all of which is not easy for them too.

🥰♡🥰♡

It is a debate that is as old as society itself. I just wrote what I believe in..

May God be kind to all the people who have lived their lives caring after their progeny.

May God bestow every child with the sensibility of love, compassion, tolerance & kindness towards their aging parents.

Why I don't WRITE...

June 11, 2020

I was too lazy to type, hence this

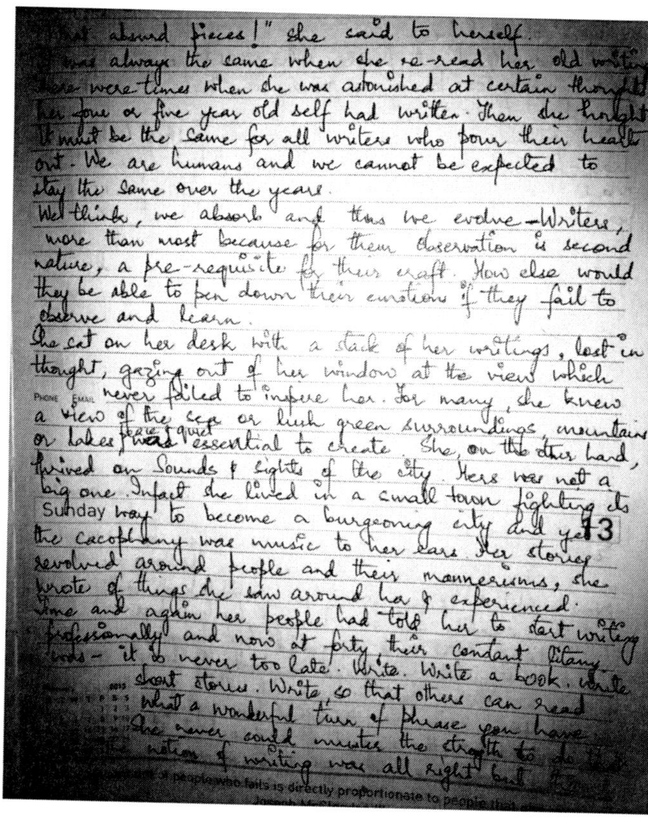

"What absurd pieces!" she said to herself.
It was always the same when she re-read her old writings.
There were times when she was astonished at certain thoughts
her four or five year old self had written. Then she thought-
It must be the same for all writers who pour their hearts
out. We are humans and we cannot be expected to
stay the same over the years.
We think, we absorb and thus we evolve—Writers,
more than most because for them observation is second
nature, a pre-requisite for their craft. How else would
they be able to pen down their emotions if they fail to
observe and learn.
She sat on her desk with a stack of her writings, lost in
thought, gazing out of her window at the view which
never failed to inspire her. For many, she knew
a view of the sea or lush green surroundings, mountains
or lakes/peace, quiet was essential to create. She, on the other hand,
thrived on sounds & sights of the city. Hers was not a
big one. Infact she lived in a small town fighting its
way to become a burgeoning city and yet
the cacophony was music to her ears. Her stories
revolved around people and their mannerisms, she
wrote of things she saw around her & experienced.
Time and again her people had told her to start writing
professionally and now at forty, their constant litany
was - it is never too late. Write. Write a book. Write
short stories. Write so that others can read
what a wonderful turn of phrase you have.
She never could muster the strength to do that.
The notion of writing was all right but ...

PAGE 1

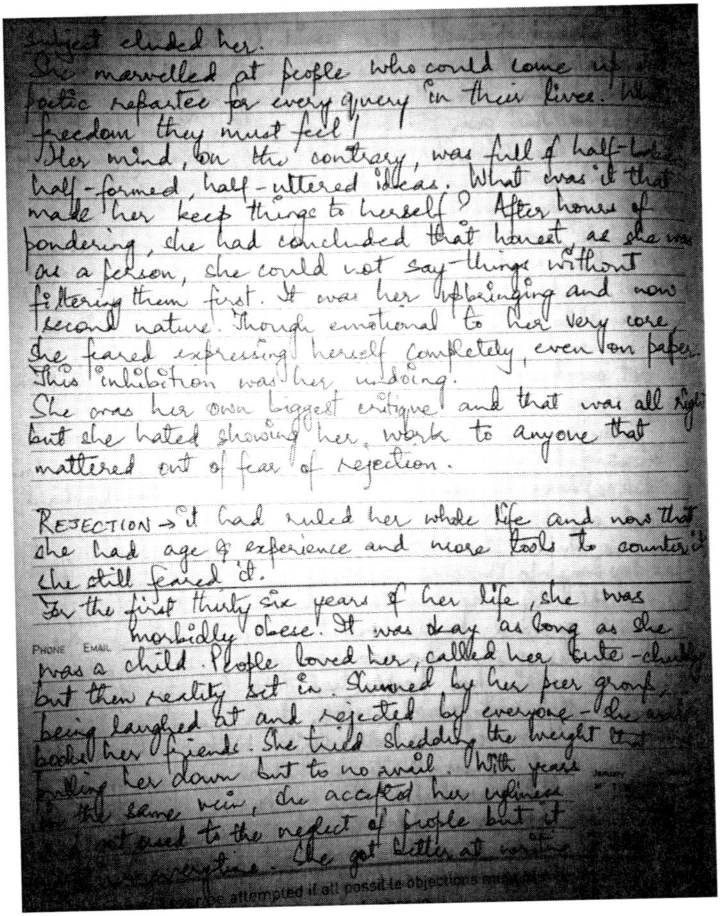
subject eluded her.
She marvelled at people who could come up with poetic repartee for every query in their lives. What freedom they must feel!
Her mind, on the contrary, was full of half-baked, half-formed, half-uttered ideas. What was it that made her keep things to herself? After hours of pondering, she had concluded that honest, as she was as a person, she could not say things without filtering them first. It was her upbringing and now second nature. Though emotional to her very core, she feared expressing herself completely, even on paper. This inhibition was her undoing.
She was her own biggest critique and that was all right but she hated showing her work to anyone that mattered out of fear of rejection.

REJECTION → it had ruled her whole life and now that she had age & experience and more tools to counter it she still feared it.
For the first thirty six years of her life, she was morbidly obese. It was okay as long as she was a child. People loved her, called her cute-chubby but then reality set in. Shunned by her peer group, being laughed at and rejected by everyone - she [illegible] books her friends. She tried shedding the weight that pulling her down but to no avail. With years [illegible] same vein, she accepted her ugliness [illegible] got used to the neglect of people but it [illegible] everything. She got better at writing

PAGE 2

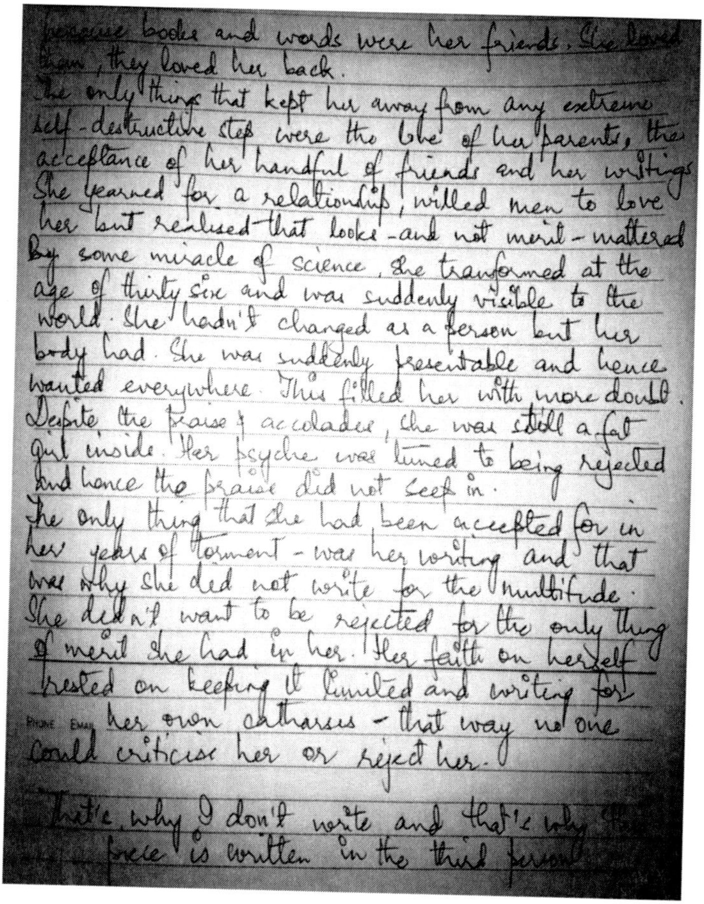
because books and words were her friends. She loved them, they loved her back.
The only thing that kept her away from any extreme self-destructive step were the love of her parents, the acceptance of her handful of friends and her writings. She yearned for a relationship, willed men to love her but realised that looks - and not merit - mattered. By some miracle of science, she transformed at the age of thirty six and was suddenly visible to the world. She hadn't changed as a person but her body had. She was suddenly presentable and hence wanted everywhere. This filled her with more doubt. Despite the praise & accolades, she was still a fat girl inside. Her psyche was tuned to being rejected and hence the praise did not seep in.
The only thing that she had been accepted for in her years of torment - was her writing and that was why she did not write for the multitude. She didn't want to be rejected for the only thing of merit she had in her. Her faith on herself rested on keeping it limited and writing for her own catharsis - that way no one could criticise her or reject her.

That's why I don't write and that's why the piece is written in the third person.

PAGE 3

Raw, honest and pathetic handwriting 😑

Home🏠

June 22, 2020

Every evening I sit and observe
People getting back from work,
Cars and bikes rushing
To the safety of their premises.
Like birds returning to their nests
After exploring fresh spaces.

Big or small,
Designed or regular,
Full or empty,
There is nothing that beckons us more.
Safety, contentment & a sense of belonging
Some find it in a place, some in a person they love♡♡

I am looking for a home..

A Free Verse

July 1, 2020

'I wish we could love in moderation',
Said her best friend.

She was reminded of her sister's words
From a few months ago.
'If only you could hate that one less
And love this one with boundaries,
You would be happy.'

It wasn't in her to dilute her emotions.
The love, the hate, the compassion, the fear
Everything ate at her
Consumed her
Made her a little less her.

But she was content for having had someone to love & cherish that much.

She did not live life by halves

It had always been 'all or nothing' for her

This time, though, God had other plans.

She was given ALL, temporarily.

The memories she tried to make were there to stay, their short creation span

The only regret…

Almosts...

July 6, 2020

How many times have you asked me-
'Almost there', where!!

How many times have you read my ink
with this rhetorical question in your tone!!
💫✨

How many times have you implied that I deserve better...
Better than you...

What you don't understand is that I don't need Perfect.
I need you.

With all your flaws, with all the shortcomings,
With all the travesties of fate,
All I really want is You.
I want us to make a life together.

There are so many things that I have adapted to, 'effortlessly',
Just so that I might share a part of you.
Your music, your indulgences, your language, your taste.
How I wish things were a little different, a little in my favor!
There are so many questions I push back because I don't want to disturb the balance.
The balance that we have forged to move ahead with our 'situation'.
Love at one end, habit on the other.
We walk a fine line between love and friendship.
'Let's call it affection', you said
Well, some say – 'that' lasts more than love. So let's try that.
I would agree to anything if it means being with you.

There are times when I 'Almost' let you go,
But then you do and say things that warm the cockles of my heart.
There are instances when you 'Almost' lose me to your indifference.

But then, you are my home. I can't go far.

And I am 'almost always' back where I started, with you as my axis.

But now I am just a little tired of the 'Almosts'

I wish I had a life where you loved me 'Almost' as much as I do.

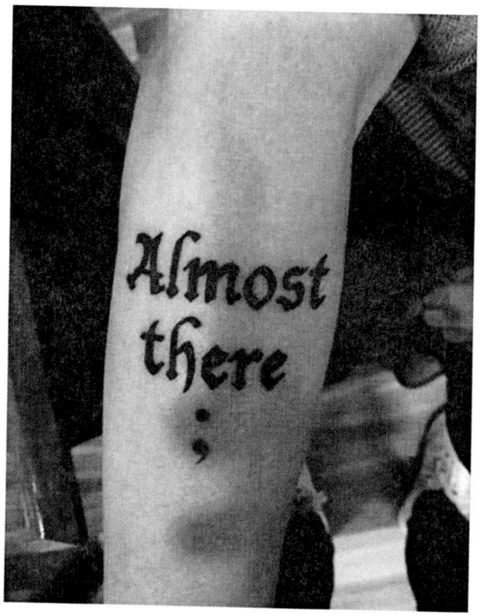

What does the Future hold?

August 28, 2020

A friend of mine wrote something about meeting different kinds of people in life, experiences gained, lessons learnt and his fears about his life and its uncertain propositions at the age of 43.

I, myself, have reached the mature age of 40. There are times when I feel old, (mostly the doings of an unhealthy lifestyle growing up) but I got to thinking and I am not fearful of the future. It is true that the age which can be called 'prime' is already past and yet there still is a lot left to do.

I am a person of meagre requirements, I can survive on basics as far as materialistic possessions are concerned. I don't need the latest in technology to feel a part of the moving, dynamic world, neither do I require branded clothing and footwear to convince myself that I am moving with the times. I can do pretty well with homemade food and long walks too. Hence, I have a pretty good picture of my future etched in my mind. It would be sedentary and I would be pleased, even if I only have my books, pen, paper in material possessions and LOVE to make everything worthwhile.

Love makes everything worthwhile

I am a romantic and I do see the world through rose – colored glasses. In these forty years I have come across loads of experiences, some pleasant, others educative. I have encountered people of every kind. Like most of us, I have seen friends who disappear once their interests are served, along side friends who appear only when needed badly and still behave the same as, may be, years before.

I am lucky to have a bunch of the latter category, although I have seen a deluge of the former. And yet my belief in the goodness of mankind never waivers. To each his or her own. As we sow, so shall we reap. If we have been good to people, that good will come back to us in unexpected ways. If someone has been nasty to us, it isn't for us to decide how they should be punished by coming down to their level. There is a system of checks and balances with the Almighty and HE keeps a record of everything. So why worry about the negative experiences.

Life is just too short to keep grudges and staying stuck in one place. Moving on should be the mantra. You feel appreciated, you move on because one cannot and should not rest on past laurels, you feel ignored, you move on because that place is clearly not for you but some other might be.

I have read so much and after a point of time things do not stick to our minds as they used to. So, while I might remember a story I read in middle school, I am most likely to forget what I read a week back. But a few years back, I read some principles of metaphysics that have stuck with me and anything I do, I test it on those principles. They have been helpful in getting me through agitated states of mind too. I particularly love the second one.

The Four(4) Principles of Metaphysics

It is not important whether you are spiritual or believe in God ....

But the four principles of metaphysics apply to all from the moment one is born and until our last breath !!

Metaphysics..

The First Principle states: "Whomsoever you encounter is the right one" ... This means that no one comes into our life by chance. Everyone who is around us, anyone with whom we interact, represents something, whether to teach us something or to help us improve a current situation.

The Second Principle states: "Whatever happened is the only thing that could have happened" ... Nothing, absolutely nothing of that which we experienced could have been any other way. Not even in the least important detail. There is no "If only I had done that differently, then it would have been different". NO .. What happened is the only thing that could have taken place and must have taken place for us to learn and evolve in order to move forward. Every single situation in life which we encounter is absolutely perfect, even when it defies our understanding and our ego.

The Third Principle states: "Each moment in which something begins is the right moment"... Everything begins at exactly the right moment, neither earlier nor later. This is because we are subconsciouly ready for the new experience or challenge.

The Fourth Principle states: "What is over, is over"

... It is very simple. When something comes to an end, it helps us evolve. Hence, enriched by the recent experience, it is better to let go and move on.

These principles mean that not even a single snowflake falls at the wrong time or the wrong place.

If we believe these, we wouldn't be fearful of what life holds for us. What is destined to happen will happen. We just have to keep moving. We just have to keep making prudent decisions which deem right to us at that point of time without thinking what if they backfire. They might. But we cannot see that happening while making our choices. So why get muddled. Just do what feels right in your heart. That is one voice we cannot ignore. More often than not, we will be rewarded in the long run.

We have a friend in need. What do we do? Help them or think if I help him today, he might be of use tomorrow.. That is a sick way of looking at things. If we call someone a friend, they should be helped without thinking what they can or might do for us. That's how human relationships work.

This year has been particularly challenging in many regards. Jobs, economy, health standards, social etiquette, everything has changed. There is a lot of uncertainty about everything these days. What remains the same is how we connect with people.

Life will go on. The world will keep moving and those, who keep pace with the change while being firmly planted in human relationships, will have nothing to worry of future.

Shun REGRETS. Stick by your decisions & choices. Do not stagnate. Change with changing situations. Never let go of HOPE. Keep moving. Have FAITH in the PRESENT.

May God be kind to all of us.

May the future hold only good things.

Clueless

March 10, 2022

When you don't know what the future holds,

When things grow stale and cold…

When you feel a void where life once had been..

It's time to come clean..

IT IS TIME TO COME CLEAN.

A Meaningful Life..

May 17, 2022

We leave pieces of ourselves in places we have been to,
with people we have loved,
in moments we have cherished
and
in pages we have read..

When we revisit, it is never the same place, thing, person or the time.

The place looks and feels different – enriched, fuller,

the people more familiar,

the moments more our own

and

the books a little thicker..

We yield a little of what we were
& yet
Grow into a little more of what we are destined to become.